ENDOMORPH DIET FOR BEGINNERS

Unlock Your Body's Hidden Potential, Burn Fat With Tailored Nutritional Strategies, Personalized Fitness, Holistic Wellness Tactics, And a 45-Day Meal Plan

MARYEM PETTERSON

Table of Contents

Introduction

Welcome to the world of health, fitness, and self-discovery! This book is specifically designed with you, the endomorph, in mind. Whether you're already on a fitness journey or just starting to explore a healthier lifestyle, this book will provide you with practical advice, valuable insights, and motivation to help you achieve your goals.

As an endomorph, you may have faced unique challenges when it comes to managing your weight and improving your overall health. But fear not! This book aims to empower you with the knowledge and tools necessary to overcome these challenges and unlock your full potential.

What Is an Endomorph?

In the 1940s, the American researcher and psychologist William Sheldon made significant contributions to our understanding of body types by introducing a classification system. Sheldon's research delved into the intricate relationship between our skeletal structure and body composition, leading him to propose the concept of somatotypes. He believed that these somatotypes are inherited and distinct to each person, serving as a crucial factor in determining whether someone has a natural inclination to be slim, carry more weight, or fall somewhere in between. This idea had profound implications for the fields of weight management and fitness, as it underscored the importance of personalized approaches to achieving health and fitness goals.

One of the somatotypes Sheldon identified is the endomorph. Endomorphs exhibit a higher proportion of body fat and relatively lower muscle mass. They tend to have a softer, rounder physique, although it's important to note that being an endomorph does not necessarily equate to obesity. Due to their specific physical makeup, individuals with endomorphic bodies often find themselves more sensitive to calorie consumption than those with different body types. This heightened sensitivity means that endomorphs must pay close attention to their dietary choices to ensure they do not inadvertently consume more calories than they burn. Additionally, endomorphs typically possess a larger frame, which can contribute to the perception that losing weight is a more challenging endeavor for them.

These characteristics set endomorphs apart from the other two primary somatotypes, ectomorphs and mesomorphs. Ectomorphs are individuals with a higher metabolism, allowing them to consume larger quantities of food with minimal weight gain. They typically have smaller joints, a smaller overall body size, and a narrower frame. This metabolic advantage often means that ectomorphs can maintain a leaner physique without putting in as much effort as individuals with different body types.

On the opposite end of the spectrum, the mesomorph somatotype falls somewhere between ectomorph and endomorph. Mesomorphs typically possess a larger skeletal frame but maintain a lower percentage of body fat. Their bodies have a propensity for gaining muscle and losing weight relatively easily, making them well-suited for endeavors like bodybuilding and athletic performance.

William Sheldon's pioneering research and the concept of somatotypes have provided valuable insights into the diversity of human body types. Endomorphs, with their unique characteristics, highlight the importance of tailoring dietary and fitness strategies to individual somatotypes. This recognition of individual variation has become a cornerstone of modern approaches to achieving and maintaining a healthy weight and overall fitness.

How to Use This Book

This book is designed to be a comprehensive guide that you can refer to throughout your fitness journey. Here's how you can make the most of it:

1. **Read it Thoroughly:** Start by reading this book from cover to cover to gain a complete understanding of endomorph physiology, health considerations, and fitness strategies.

2. **Refer Back:** Use this book as a reference guide. Whenever you have questions or need guidance, come back to specific chapters or sections that address your concerns.

3. **Act:** Knowledge alone won't lead to transformation. Apply what you learn from this book to your daily life. Experiment with different fitness routines, dietary changes, and lifestyle adjustments.

4. **Connect with Others:** Consider joining fitness communities or support groups, either in person or online, where you can share your experiences, seek advice, and find encouragement from others on a similar journey.

Motivation, Courage and Perseverance

Embarking on a fitness and health journey can be daunting, especially when you're faced with unique challenges as an endomorph. However, remember that motivation, courage, and perseverance are key ingredients for success.

Motivation: Understand why you want to make changes in your life. Is it to improve your overall health, boost your confidence, or simply feel better in your body? Your motivation will be your driving force on tough days.

Courage: Initiating something new, venturing beyond your comfort zone, and confronting possible obstacles require a significant amount of courage. Courage means embracing change and believing in your ability to transform.

Perseverance: Achieving a healthy body is a gradual process that demands persistence. There will be setbacks and plateaus along the way, but perseverance means staying committed to your goals and continuing to push forward, even when progress seems slow.

Your path as an endomorph is distinct, yet with determination and proper guidance, you can attain remarkable outcomes.

Understanding Your Body

To make meaningful changes in your life, it's essential to understand your body. This includes recognizing your body type, metabolic rate, and how your genetics influence your physique. By gaining insight into your body, you can tailor your fitness and nutrition strategies for maximum effectiveness.

The Three Body Types

Understanding your body and its various body types is essential for maintaining good health and making informed decisions about your lifestyle and fitness. Let's explore the three body types: Apple-shaped endomorph, Pear-shaped endomorph, and Athletic endomorph.

Apple-Shaped Endomorph

Apple-shaped endomorphs typically have a rounder or oval-shaped body with more fat accumulation around the abdominal area. They may have broader shoulders and a narrower lower body.

This body type is associated with a higher risk of certain health problems, primarily due to the presence of visceral fat (fat stored deep within the abdomen). These health issues can encompass conditions such as type 2 diabetes, heart disease, hypertension, and metabolic syndrome.

To mitigate health risks, apple-shaped endomorphs should focus on both cardiovascular exercise to burn calories and resistance training to build muscle. A well-balanced diet that emphasizes portion control and whole, nutrient-dense foods is essential for managing weight and reducing visceral fat.

Pear-Shaped Endomorph

Pear-shaped endomorphs typically have a narrower upper body and tend to accumulate excess fat in the hip, thigh, and buttock areas. This body type is often referred to as the "pear" or "triangle" shape.

While pear-shaped individuals may have a lower risk of some health issues compared to apple-shaped endomorphs, they may still face challenges related to body image and self-esteem. Fat stored in the lower body can be stubborn and challenging to lose.

To achieve a balanced physique and improve overall health, pear-shaped endomorphs should focus on a combination of cardiovascular exercise and strength training. Targeting exercises for the lower body can help tone and strengthen these areas. Emphasis on a balanced diet is crucial for sustainable weight management.

Athletic Endomorph

Athletic endomorphs have a more muscular and stocky build. They tend to gain muscle relatively easily but may also accumulate fat if not careful with their diet and exercise routine.

While athletic endomorphs may have a metabolic advantage when it comes to building muscle, they should be mindful of diet and exercise to prevent excessive fat gain. Maintaining a healthy body composition is key.

Athletic endomorphs often excel in strength-based sports and activities. They should focus on a well-rounded fitness routine that includes strength training, cardiovascular exercise, and flexibility work. Maintaining a balanced diet that promotes the growth and preservation of muscles is crucial.

Understanding your specific body type is the first step toward tailoring your fitness and nutrition plans to address your unique strengths and challenges. It's important to remember that individual variations exist within each body type, and genetics is just one factor in the equation. Remaining steadfast in healthy practices, which encompass regular physical activity and a well-balanced diet, is the cornerstone of attaining and sustaining optimal health and well-being, irrespective of your body type. Consulting with fitness and nutrition professionals can provide personalized guidance for your specific goals and needs.

The Role of Genetics

Genetics, the inheritance of traits from your parents, is like the blueprint that shapes your body. Here are some ways in which genetics influence your body:

• **Body Type:** Your genetic makeup largely determines your body type, whether you have an ectomorph (slim), mesomorph (muscular), or endomorph (curvy or round) physique. These body types dictate how you naturally store and distribute fat and muscle.

• **Metabolism:** Your basal metabolic rate (BMR), which is the number of calories your body burns at rest, is influenced by genetics. Some people have a naturally faster metabolism, allowing them to burn calories more quickly, while others have a slower metabolism and may be more prone to weight gain.

• **Muscle Mass Potential:** Genetics also play a role in determining your muscle mass potential. Some individuals have a genetic advantage in building and maintaining muscle, while others may need to put in more effort to achieve similar results.

• **Health Predispositions:** Genetic factors can increase your susceptibility to certain health conditions. For example, if your family has a history of heart disease, diabetes, or certain cancers, you may be genetically predisposed to these conditions.

Working with Your Genetics

While you can't change your genetic makeup, you can work with it to achieve your fitness and health goals:

• **Tailored Workouts:** Understanding your body type and genetic predispositions can help you design a workout plan that aligns with your natural strengths and challenges. For instance, if you're naturally muscular (mesomorph), you might excel in strength training.

- **Nutrition:** Your genetics can influence how your body processes and stores nutrients. By knowing your genetic tendencies, you can make informed dietary choices to optimize your health. For example, if you have a genetic predisposition to high cholesterol, you might focus on a heart-healthy diet.

- **Health Monitoring:** Genetic testing can provide insights into your susceptibility to certain diseases or conditions. This information can guide you in making proactive health choices, such as regular check-ups and early interventions.

The Impact of Lifestyle Choices

It's crucial to recognize that genetics are just one piece of the puzzle in your health and fitness journey. Lifestyle choices play a significant role:

- **Nutrition:** Your dietary choices wield significant influence over your well-being. Adopting a well-balanced diet tailored to meet your nutritional requirements can aid in sustaining a healthy weight and mitigating health risks, even in the presence of genetic predispositions.

- **Physical Activity:** Consistent engagement in physical activities can facilitate the attainment and maintenance of a healthy weight, enhance muscle strength, elevate metabolism, and reduce the likelihood of chronic illnesses, irrespective of your genetic makeup.

- **Rest:** Sufficient sleep is a fundamental component of overall health. Inadequate sleep can detrimentally affect metabolism, appetite regulation, and mental well-being, regardless of your genetic background.

- **Stress Management:** Prolonged stress can have adverse health consequences. Effective stress management techniques can help alleviate these effects and enhance your overall quality of life, regardless of genetic factors.

While genetics do play a significant role in determining various aspects of your body and health, they are not the sole determining factor. Your lifestyle choices, including diet, exercise, sleep, and stress management, have a powerful influence on your overall well-being and can help you optimize your health, regardless of your genetic predispositions. It's about working in harmony with your genes to lead a healthy and fulfilling life.

Connection Between Endomorphs and Health Problems

Endomorphs, especially those with an apple-shaped body, do face some unique health risks due to their body composition and fat distribution. It's important to understand these risks and take proactive steps to mitigate them:

1. **Heart Disease:** Excess fat around the midsection, often referred to as visceral fat, is associated with an increased risk of heart disease. This type of fat is metabolically active and can release substances that contribute to inflammation and atherosclerosis (the buildup of plaque in arteries).

2. **Type 2 Diabetes:** Apple-shaped endomorphs may be more prone to insulin resistance, a condition where cells do not respond effectively to insulin. This can result in heightened blood sugar levels, consequently raising the likelihood of developing type 2 diabetes.

3. **High Blood Pressure:** Obesity, which can be more prevalent in endomorphs, is a significant risk factor for hypertension (high blood pressure). Excess body fat can strain the cardiovascular system and lead to elevated blood pressure levels.

4. **Joint Issues:** Carrying excess weight places additional stress on the joints, particularly those in the knees, hips, and lower back. Over time, this can lead to joint problems, pain, and an increased risk of conditions like osteoarthritis.

5. **Sleep Apnea:** Obesity is a common concern for endomorphs, and it is a significant risk factor for sleep apnea. Sleep apnea is a sleep disorder marked by interruptions in breathing during sleep, leading to disrupted sleep patterns and potentially severe health issues, such as daytime fatigue and an elevated risk of cardiovascular problems.

Mitigating Health Risks:

While these potential health concerns may seem daunting, it's crucial to remember that they are not inevitable or insurmountable. There are several proactive steps individuals, especially endomorphs, can take to mitigate these risks and lead a healthier, happier life:

1. **Healthy Nutrition:** Adopting a balanced diet that includes a variety of vegetables, fruits, lean proteins, whole grains, and healthy fats can help manage weight, reduce inflammation, and improve metabolic health.

2. **Consistent Exercise:** Incorporating regular physical activity into your routine, which includes both cardiovascular workouts like brisk walking or cycling, as well as strength training, can assist in weight control, enhance insulin sensitivity, and fortify your cardiovascular system.

3. **Weight Maintenance:** Attaining and sustaining a healthy body weight plays a pivotal role in diminishing the hazards linked to excess body fat. Gradual and sustainable weight management can significantly enhance overall well-being.

4. **Stress Reduction:** Persistent stress can lead to unhealthy lifestyle choices and exacerbate health issues. Employing stress management methods such as meditation, yoga, or counseling can be beneficial.

5. **Sleep Habits:** Giving importance to good sleep practices, such as adhering to a consistent sleep schedule and establishing a comfortable sleeping environment, can enhance sleep quality and diminish the likelihood of developing sleep apnea.

6. **Regular Health Check-ups:** Periodic medical examinations can assist in monitoring vital health indicators such as blood pressure and blood sugar levels. Early identification and control of risk factors are essential for averting complications.

While endomorphs, particularly those with an apple-shaped body, may face an increased risk of certain health problems, proactive lifestyle choices can have a significant impact on reducing these risks and promoting long-term health and well-being. Consulting with healthcare professionals and registered dietitians can provide personalized guidance and support on the journey to a healthier life.

The Basics of the Diet

What Is the Diet for Endomorphs

There has been considerable discussion surrounding the endomorph weight loss diet. Irrespective of one's body type, weight loss can be achieved by expending more calories than one consumes. However, if you possess an endomorph body type and aspire to reduce weight or enhance muscle definition, it is advisable to adopt a tailored workout regimen and diet designed for individuals with the same body type.

The underlying theory behind this diet suggests that endomorphs have a metabolism that operates at a slower pace compared to ectomorphs. Due to this reduced metabolic rate, excess calorie intake can result in fat storage, especially when contrasted with ectomorphs and mesomorphs. Furthermore, experts contend that endomorphs may have a diminished capacity to digest and utilize carbohydrates effectively. Therefore, an ideal diet for this body type may emphasize a higher consumption of fats and proteins while limiting carbohydrate intake. A notable example of such a diet is the paleo diet, which facilitates fat loss while maintaining energy levels.

An endomorph diet, which prioritizes lean protein, healthy fats, and complex carbohydrates while minimizing simple carbs, represents one viable option. This dietary approach shares elements with the paleo, Mediterranean, and keto diets. To achieve this, you can reduce your daily carbohydrate intake by 30% or replace unhealthy carbohydrates with fiber-rich whole grains that also provide sustained energy. The remaining 70% should be divided between protein and healthy fats. It is advisable to focus on incorporating fruits, vegetables, lean meats, fish, nuts, and seeds into your diet. Balancing protein, healthy fats, fiber-rich foods, and selecting healthy carbohydrates should be equally emphasized. While doing so, it's important to keep portion sizes smaller than usual to prevent excessive hunger that may lead to overeating during subsequent meals.

Macronutrients Explained

Macronutrients constitute the fundamental constituents of your diet, supplying the energy and essential nutrients necessary for your body to operate at its best. For individuals with an endomorph body type, making informed choices about macronutrients is particularly crucial in achieving their health and fitness goals.

Carbohydrates: Carbohydrates are the primary fuel source for your body's energy needs. As an endomorph, it's essential to be mindful of the types of carbohydrates you consume. Opting for complex carbohydrates, such as whole grains, legumes, and a variety of vegetables, is highly advisable over simple sugars. Complex carbohydrates offer a sustained release of energy, which not only fuels your body but also helps in stabilizing blood sugar levels. This stability in blood sugar reduces the temptation to overeat and contributes to better control over your overall calorie intake.

Proteins: Proteins serve as the fundamental building blocks for various components of your body, making them a critical part of your diet, especially if you're an endomorph. Prioritize lean sources of protein, which can be found in foods like chicken, turkey, fish, lean cuts of beef or pork, tofu, and legumes. Including these protein sources in your meals is vital for several reasons. Firstly, protein plays a significant role in preserving and even increasing muscle mass. Given that muscle mass directly impacts your metabolism, maintaining or enhancing it can be instrumental in your efforts to manage your weight effectively. Additionally, protein has the remarkable ability to keep you feeling satisfied and full for extended periods, reducing the likelihood of unnecessary snacking and overindulging.

Fats: While it may seem counterintuitive, fats, specifically the healthy varieties, are a crucial component of a well-balanced diet, even for endomorphs. Healthy fats, such as monounsaturated and polyunsaturated fats, are abundant in foods like avocados, nuts, seeds, and olive oil. These fats not only include delightful flavors to your meals but also offer significant health benefits. They play a pivotal role in promoting heart health and can leave you feeling satiated after eating. By incorporating these healthy fats into your diet, you can also facilitate portion control, making it easier to manage your overall calorie intake.

Portion Control for Endomorphs

Portion control is a crucial aspect of managing calorie intake and achieving and maintaining a healthy weight, especially for individuals with an endomorph body type. Endomorphs often have a genetic predisposition to store excess calories as fat, making portion control particularly relevant for them. Here are some effective strategies for practicing portion control:

7. **Use Smaller Plates:** Eating off smaller plates can create a visual illusion of larger portion sizes, tricking your brain into feeling more satisfied with less food. This can help prevent overeating and promote mindful consumption.

8. **Measure Your Food:** Investing in measuring teacups and a kitchen scale is a practical way to accurately portion your meals, especially when cooking at home. Measuring ingredients allows you to control calorie intake and maintain awareness of portion sizes.

9. **Practice Mindful Eating:** Be mindful of your body's hunger and fullness signals. Consuming food at a leisurely pace and relishing each bite can aid in avoiding overeating. Put your fork down between bites and engage all your senses in the eating experience.

10. **Avoid Eating Directly from Containers:** Eating directly from a box of cookies, a bag of chips, or a large container of food can lead to mindless eating, where you consume more than intended.

Instead, portion out a serving size onto a plate or into a small bowl to create a clear visual representation of your portion.

11. **Learn Serving Sizes:** Familiarize yourself with standard serving sizes for different types of food. This knowledge can help you estimate portions when dining out or when nutritional information is not readily available. For example, a serving of lean meat is typically the size of a deck of cards.

12. **Pre-Portion Snacks:** When you purchase snacks in bulk, take the time to portion them into small containers or bags ahead of time. This proactive approach makes it easier to grab a controlled portion when you're hungry, reducing the temptation to overindulge in larger quantities.

13. **Be Mindful of Liquid Calories:** Beverages, including sugary drinks and alcoholic beverages, can contribute significant calories to your diet. Use smaller glasses or teacups for calorie-dense liquids, and consider alternatives like water, herbal tea, or flavored water with no added sugars.

14. **Practice Self-Awareness:** Regularly assess your portion sizes and eating habits. Keep a food journal to track what you eat and drink, as well as your portion sizes. This can help you identify areas where you may need to improve portion control.

15. **Seek Support:** Consider working with a registered dietitian or nutritionist who can provide personalized guidance on portion control and meal planning tailored to your specific needs and goals.

Practicing portion control is a valuable tool for endomorphs and individuals of all body types to manage calorie intake, achieve weight-related goals, and promote overall health. By implementing these strategies, you can develop healthy eating habits that support your well-being and help you reach and maintain a healthy weight.

Why Meal Timing Matters

Meal timing is a critical aspect of your diet, especially if you're an endomorph, as it can have a significant impact on your metabolism, energy levels, and overall health. Here's a closer look at how meal timing can benefit individuals with this body type:

Breakfast

Commencing your day with a balanced breakfast is vital. A comprehensive morning meal should encompass a combination of carbohydrates, proteins, and nutritious fats. This combination helps kickstart your metabolism after the overnight fasting period and provides sustained energy throughout the morning. By eating a nutritious breakfast, you reduce the likelihood of overeating later in the day.

Example Breakfast: Consider options like oatmeal with nuts and berries, a spinach and mushroom omelet, or whole-grain toast with avocado and scrambled eggs.

Snacking

Snacks can be a valuable part of your diet, but it's crucial to choose them wisely. As an endomorph, opt for snacks that blend protein and fiber to keep you feeling full and prevent energy crashes between meals. Avoid sugary snacks, which can lead to energy spikes and crashes.

Healthy Snack Ideas: Greek yogurt with berries, a handful of almonds, carrot sticks with hummus, or a small apple with peanut butter.

Lunch and Dinner

Distributing your calorie intake uniformly between lunch and dinner can help with weight management. Eating a substantial lunch can prevent excessive evening snacking, which can be a challenge for endomorphs. Aim to incorporate lean proteins, plenty of vegetables, and whole grains into your meals for balanced nutrition.

Balanced Meals: Consider meals like grilled chicken with quinoa and roasted vegetables, or a lentil and vegetable stir-fry with brown rice.

Meal Timing for Weight Loss

Some endomorphs find success with strategies like intermittent fasting. This approach involves limiting the hrs during which you eat, typically by extending the overnight fasting period and having a smaller eating window during the day. Intermittent fasting has the potential to regulate calorie consumption and enhance insulin sensitivity, offering potential benefits for weight control.

Intermittent Fasting Options: You have various options, such as the 16/8 method (fasting for 16 hrs & eating within an 8-hour window) or the 5:2 method (maintaining a regular diet for 5 days and reducing calorie intake on 2 non-consecutive days).

Late-Night Eating

Avoid consuming large meals right prior to bedtime. Consuming food shortly prior to bedtime can contribute to weight gain because your body's metabolic rate naturally decreases during sleep. If you find yourself hungry in the evening, opt for a light, protein-rich snack to satisfy your hunger without overloading your digestive system.

Healthy Evening Snacks: Consider options like a small serving of Greek yogurt, cottage cheese, a handful of mixed nuts, or a piece of string cheese.

Meal timing is a valuable tool for endomorphs, helping to regulate energy levels, control calorie intake, and support weight management efforts. By paying attention to when you eat and choosing nutrient-dense foods, you can optimize your diet for your body type and promote overall health and well-being. Remember that individual preferences and lifestyles vary, so it's important to find a meal timing strategy that works best for you and is sustainable in the long term.

Hydration and Calorie Management

Proper hydration is a fundamental aspect of maintaining overall health, and it can have a significant impact on calorie management and your diet. Here's a closer look at how hydration affects your dietary choices and overall well-being:

• **Thirst vs. Hunger:** Many times, the signals for thirst and hunger can be confusing. When you feel the urge to eat, it's possible that you're actually thirsty. Prior to automatically reaching for a snack, try drinking a glass of water first. Wait a couple of mins to see if your feelings of hunger subside. You might find that a simple glass of water can satisfy your body's needs without unnecessary calorie consumption.

• **Hydration and Metabolism:** Staying adequately hydrated is vital for supporting your metabolism. Dehydration can slow down metabolic processes, making it more challenging for your body to efficiently burn calories. When your body is properly hydrated, it functions optimally, and this can help in maintaining a healthy weight.

• **Calorie-Free Beverage Options:** Opt for calorie-free or low-calorie beverages to stay hydrated without adding extra calories to your diet. Water is, of course, the best choice for hydration without any calories or additives. Herbal teas & black coffee (without added sugar and cream) are also excellent options that can provide flavor and hydration without a calorie overload.

• **Monitor Sugary Drinks:** Exercise caution when it comes to sugary beverages like soda, fruit juices, and energy drinks. These beverages often contain substantial quantities of added sugars and provide empty calories. Overindulging in sugary drinks can lead to weight gain and increase the risk of chronic health problems like type 2 diabetes, obesity, and dental complications. Opt for healthier alternatives like water infused with fruits or vegetables for flavor or unsweetened herbal teas.

Tips for Staying Hydrated and Managing Calories:

• **Set a Hydration Schedule:** Make it a habit to drink water throughout the day. Setting specific times for hydration, such as drinking a glass of water prior to each meal or having a water bottle with you during the day, can help ensure you stay adequately hydrated.

• **Track Your Intake:** Keep track of your daily fluid intake to ensure you're meeting your hydration needs. There are apps and journals available that can help you monitor your water consumption.

• **Listen to Your Body:** Pay attention to your body's signals for thirst. If you're thirsty, reach for water instead of high-calorie beverages or snacks.

• **Incorporate Hydrating Foods:** Certain foods, such as fruits and vegetables, boast a substantial water content, making them valuable contributors to your overall hydration. Including these foods in your diet can be both a flavorful and healthful approach to maintaining adequate hydration.

Breakfast Recipes

1. Oatmeal with Almonds and Berries

Preparation time: 5 mins

Cooking time: 5 mins

Servings: 2

Ingredients:

- 1 teacup old-fashioned oats
- 2 teacups unsweetened almond milk
- 1/4 teacup sliced almonds
- 1/2 teacup mixed berries (e.g., raspberries, blackberries)
- 1 tsp honey (optional)

Directions:

1. Inside your saucepot, raise almond milk to a simmer.

2. Stir in the oats then cook for 3-5 mins till the mixture thickens.

3. Split the oatmeal into containers.

4. Top with sliced almonds and mixed berries.

5. Spray with honey if wanted.

6. Serve warm.

Per serving: Calories: 250kcal; Fat: 9g; Carbs: 35g; Protein: 8g

2. Avocado and Egg Toast

Preparation time: 5 mins

Cooking time: 5 mins

Servings: 2

Ingredients:

- 2 slices whole-grain bread
- 1 ripe avocado
- 2 big eggs
- Salt and pepper as required
- Salsa or hot sauce for garnish (optional)

Directions:

1. Toast the whole-grain bread slices.

2. While toasting, mash the ripe avocado and season using salt and pepper.

3. Fry two eggs to your desired doneness in a non-stick skillet.

4. Disperse the mashed avocado uniformly on the toasted bread.

5. Place one fried egg on each slice.

6. Include salsa or hot sauce for extra flavor if wanted.

7. Serve instantly.

Per serving: Calories: 250kcal; Fat: 12g; Carbs: 25g; Protein: 12g

3. Spinach and Mushroom Omelet

Preparation time: 5 mins

Cooking time: 10 mins

Servings: 1

Ingredients:

- 2 big eggs
- 1/2 teacup fresh spinach, severed
- 1/4 teacup mushrooms, sliced
- Salt and pepper as required
- Small amount of olive oil

Directions:

1. Warm your non-stick griddle inside a middling temp. then lightly coat it using olive oil.

2. Include sliced mushrooms then sauté for 2-3 mins 'til they start to brown.

3. Include your severed spinach then cook for an extra 2 mins till wilted.

4. Inside your container, whisk the eggs, season using salt & pepper, then pour them into your griddle with the vegetables.

5. Cook till the eggs are set and fold the omelet in half.

6. Serve warm.

Per serving: Calories: 180kcal; Fat: 12g; Carbs: 3g; Protein: 14g

4. Cottage Cheese and Veggie Wrap

Preparation time: 10 mins

Servings: 1

Ingredients:

- 1 whole-grain tortilla
- 1/2 teacup low-fat cottage cheese
- 1/4 teacup cubed bell peppers
- 1/4 teacup cubed cucumber
- 1/4 teacup baby spinach leaves
- Salt and pepper as required

Directions:

1. Lay the whole-grain tortilla flat.

2. Disperse the cottage cheese uniformly over the tortilla.

3. Sprinkle cubed bell peppers and cucumber on top.

4. Include baby spinach leaves.

5. Season using salt and pepper.

6. Roll the tortilla tightly, cut in half, and serve.

Per serving: Calories: 250kcal; Fat: 6g; Carbs: 30g; Protein: 18g

5. Sweet Potato and Spinach Hash

Preparation time: 10 mins

Cooking time: 15 mins

Servings: 2

Ingredients:

- 1 large sweet potato, skinned and cubed
- 1 teacup fresh spinach leaves
- 1/2 red bell pepper, cubed
- 2 eggs
- Salt and pepper as required
- Olive oil for cooking

Directions:

1. Heat your skillet inside a middling temp. then include a small amount of olive oil.

2. Include cubed sweet potato then sauté 'til they start to brown and become soft, about 10-12 mins.

3. Include cubed bell pepper then cook for an extra 2-3 mins.

4. Stir in fresh spinach then cook till wilted.

5. Push the veggies aside and crack the eggs into your griddle. Cook 'til the egg whites are set but the yolks are still runny.

6. Season using salt and pepper and serve.

Per serving: Calories: 220kcal; Fat: 8g; Carbs: 30g; Protein: 10g

6. Berry and Nut Butter Wrap

Preparation time: 5 mins

Servings: 1

Ingredients:

- 1 whole-grain tortilla
- 2 tbsps almond or cashew butter (no added sugar)
- 1/2 teacup mixed berries (e.g., raspberries, blueberries)
- 1 tbsp chia seeds (optional)

Directions:

1. Lay the whole-grain tortilla flat.

2. Disperse almond or cashew butter uniformly over the tortilla.

3. Include mixed berries on top.

4. Sprinkle chia seeds if wanted.

5. Roll the tortilla tightly, cut in half, and serve.

Per serving: Calories: 320kcal; Fat: 17g; Carbs: 35g; Protein: 9g

7. Turkey and Veggie Breakfast Burrito

Preparation time: 10 mins

Cooking time: 10 mins

Servings: 2

Ingredients:

- 4 big eggs
- 1/2 teacup cubed turkey breast (cooked)
- 1/2 teacup cubed bell peppers
- 1/4 teacup cubed onions
- 1/4 teacup shredded low-fat cheese
- Salt and pepper as required
- 2 whole-grain tortillas

Directions:

1. Inside your container, whisk the eggs and season using salt and pepper.

2. Warm your non-stick griddle inside a middling temp. then include a small amount of olive oil.

3. Include cubed onions and bell peppers then sauté for 2-3 mins.

4. Bring the whisked eggs into your griddle and scramble till cooked.

5. Split the cooked eggs, turkey, and shredded cheese between the two tortillas.

6. Roll each tortilla, folding in the sides, to create a burrito.

7. Serve warm.

Per serving: Calories: 320kcal; Fat: 12g; Carbs: 25g; Protein: 25g

8. Berry and Spinach Smoothie Bowl

Preparation time: 10 mins

Servings: 1

Ingredients:

- 1 teacup fresh spinach leaves
- 1/2 teacup mixed berries (e.g., strawberries, blueberries)
- 1/2 banana
- 1/2 teacup unsweetened almond milk
- 1 tbsp chia seeds (optional)
- Toppings (e.g., sliced almonds, shredded coconut)

Directions:

1. Inside a mixer, blend fresh spinach, mixed berries, banana, almond milk, and chia seeds (if wanted).

2. Blend till smooth.

3. Pour the smoothie into a container.

4. Top using sliced almonds and shredded coconut, or your preferred toppings.

5. Relish!

Per serving: Calories: 280kcal; Fat: 10g; Carbs: 45g; Protein: 7g

9. Veggie and Turkey Sausage Breakfast Casserole

Preparation time: 15 mins

Cooking time: 35 mins

Servings: 4

Ingredients:

- 4 turkey sausage links, cubed
- 1 teacup cubed bell peppers (any color)
- 1 teacup cubed onions
- 1 teacup baby spinach leaves
- 6 large eggs
- 1/2 teacup low-fat milk
- Salt and pepper as required

Directions:

1. Warm up your oven to 350 deg.F.

2. Inside an oven-safe griddle, cook the cubed turkey sausage till browned. Take out and put away.

3. Inside your similar griddle, include cubed bell peppers and onions. Sauté 'til they begin to soften. Stir in baby spinach leaves then cook till wilted.

4. Inside your container, whisk collectively eggs, milk, salt, and pepper.

5. Transfer the egg mixture over the veggies and sausage in the griddle.

6. Cook on the stovetop for a couple of mins till the edges start to set.

7. Handover the griddle to the warmed up oven then bake for around 20-25 mins till the center is fully cooked. Slice into wedges and serve.

Per serving: Calories: 280kcal; Fat: 12g; Carbs: 14g; Protein: 24g

10. Cottage Cheese Pancakes

Preparation time: 10 mins

Cooking time: 10 mins

Servings: 2 (6 small pancakes)

Ingredients:

- 1 teacup low-fat cottage cheese
- 2 big eggs
- 1/4 teacup oat flour (blend rolled oats to make your own)
- 1/2 tsp vanilla extract
- Small amount of olive oil

Directions:

1. Inside a mixer, blend cottage cheese, eggs, oat flour, and vanilla extract. Blend till smooth.

2. Warm your non-stick griddle inside a middling temp. then lightly coat it using olive oil.

3. Pour small portions of the batter onto your griddle to make pancakes.

4. Cook for 2-3 mins on all sides till golden brown.

5. Serve.

Per serving: Calories: 250kcal; Fat: 7g; Carbs: 18g; Protein: 27g

11. Spinach and Feta Breakfast Wrap

Preparation time: 10 mins

Cooking time: 5 mins

Servings: 1

Ingredients:

- 1 whole-grain tortilla
- 2 big eggs
- 1/2 teacup fresh spinach leaves
- 2 tbsps crumbled feta cheese
- Salt and pepper as required
- Small amount of olive oil

Directions:

1. Warm your non-stick griddle inside a middling temp. then lightly coat it using olive oil.

2. Scramble the eggs in the griddle 'til they are cooked to your liking.

3. Put your whole-grain tortilla on a plate.

4. Lay fresh spinach leaves on the tortilla.

5. Spoon the scrambled eggs on top.

6. Sprinkle with crumbled feta cheese.

7. Season using salt and pepper.

8. Roll the tortilla, cut in half, and serve.

Per serving: Calories: 350kcal; Fat: 20g; Carbs: 25g; Protein: 20g

12. Overnight Chia Seed Pudding with Berries

Preparation time: 5 mins (plus chilling time)

Servings: 2

Ingredients:

- 1/2 teacup chia seeds
- 2 teacups unsweetened almond milk
- 1 tsp vanilla extract
- 1 teacup mixed berries (e.g., raspberries, strawberries)

Directions:

1. Inside your container, blend chia seeds, almond milk, and vanilla extract.

2. Stir thoroughly, cover, and put in the fridge for almost 4 hrs or overnight, stirring occasionally.

3. Prior to serving, divide the pudding into two containers.

4. Top with mixed berries.

5. Relish!

Per serving: Calories: 200kcal; Fat: 11g; Carbs: 21g; Protein: 6g

13. Quinoa Breakfast Bowl

Preparation time: 5 mins

Cooking time: 15 mins

Servings: 2

Ingredients:

• 1 teacup cooked quinoa

• 1/2 teacup sliced strawberries

• 1/2 teacup sliced bananas

• 1/4 teacup severed nuts (e.g., almonds, pecans)

• 1/4 teacup unsweetened Greek yogurt

• 1 tbsp honey (optional)

Directions:

1. Inside your container, divide the cooked quinoa into two portions.

2. Top with sliced strawberries and bananas.

3. Include your severed nuts and a dollop of Greek yogurt.

4. Spray with honey if wanted.

5. Relish!

Per serving: Calories: 300kcal; Fat: 12g; Carbs: 40g; Protein: 10g

14. Chia Seed Pudding

Preparation time: 5 mins (plus chilling time)

Servings: 2

Ingredients:

• 1/4 teacup chia seeds

• 1 teacup unsweetened almond milk

• 1/2 tsp vanilla extract

• 1 tbsp honey (optional)

• Fresh berries for topping

Directions:

1. Inside your container, blend chia seeds, almond milk, vanilla extract, and honey (if wanted).

2. Stir thoroughly, cover, and put in the fridge for almost 4 hrs or overnight.

3. Prior to serving, stir the pudding to ensure an even consistency.

4. Top with fresh berries prior to serving.

Per serving: Calories: 150kcal; Fat: 7g; Carbs: 15g; Protein: 5g

15. Smoked Salmon and Avocado Toast

Preparation time: 5 mins

Servings: 1

Ingredients:

- 2 slices whole-grain bread
- 2 oz. smoked salmon
- 1/2 ripe avocado, sliced
- 1 tsp lemon juice
- Fresh dill for garnish (optional)

Directions:

1. Toast the whole-grain bread slices.

2. Mash the sliced avocado with lemon juice.

3. Disperse the mashed avocado uniformly over the toasted bread.

4. Arrange the smoked salmon on top.

5. Garnish using fresh dill if wanted.

6. Serve instantly.

Per serving: Calories: 320kcal; Fat: 18g; Carbs: 25g; Protein: 18g

16. Greek Yogurt and Berry Parfait with Almonds

Preparation time: 5 mins

Servings: 1

Ingredients:

- 1 teacup plain Greek yogurt
- 1/2 teacup mixed berries (e.g., blueberries, raspberries)
- 1/4 teacup sliced almonds
- 1 tbsp honey (optional)

Directions:

1. Inside a glass or container, start with a layer of Greek yogurt.

2. Put your layer of mixed berries on top.

3. Sprinkle sliced almonds on the berries.

4. Spray with honey if wanted.

5. Repeat layers if wanted.

6. Relish!

Per serving: Calories: 350kcal; Fat: 15g; Carbs: 30g; Protein: 25g

17. Veggie Scramble

Preparation time: 5 mins

Cooking time: 10 mins

Servings: 2

Ingredients:

- 4 big eggs
- 1/2 bell pepper, cubed
- 1/2 onion, severed
- 1/2 teacup spinach, severed
- Salt and pepper as required
- Small amount of olive oil

Directions:

1. Warm your non-stick griddle inside a middling temp. then lightly coat it using olive oil.

2. Include your severed bell pepper and onion to your griddle. Sauté for 2-3 mins 'til they start to soften.

3. Include your severed spinach then cook for an extra 2 mins till wilted.

4. Inside your container, whisk the eggs, season using salt & pepper, then pour them into your griddle with the vegetables.

5. Stir continuously 'til the eggs are cooked to your desired consistency.

6. Serve warm.

Per serving: Calories: 150kcal; Fat: 10g; Carbs: 6g; Protein: 11g

18. Spinach and Mushroom Breakfast Quesadilla

Preparation time: 10 mins

Cooking time: 10 mins

Servings: 2

Ingredients:

- 4 whole-grain tortillas
- 2 teacups fresh spinach leaves
- 1 teacup sliced mushrooms
- 1/2 teacup shredded low-fat cheese
- Salt and pepper as required
- Small amount of olive oil

Directions:

1. Inside your griddle, heat a small amount of olive oil inside a middling temp.

2. Include sliced mushrooms then sauté 'til they start to brown.

3. Stir in fresh spinach leaves then cook till wilted.

4. Take out the veggies from the griddle then put away.

5. Place one tortilla in the griddle and spray half of the shredded cheese on it.

6. Include half of the spinach and mushroom mixture on top.

7. Top with another tortilla and press gently.

8. Cook for 2-3 mins on all sides till the quesadilla is golden brown and the cheese is dissolved.

9. Repeat the process for the second quesadilla.

10. Cut each quesadilla into wedges and serve.

Per serving: Calories: 300kcal; Fat: 10g; Carbs: 40g; Protein: 15g

19. Almond Butter and Banana Smoothie

Preparation time: 5 mins

Servings: 1

Ingredients:

- 1 ripe banana
- 2 tbsps almond butter (no added sugar)
- 1 teacup unsweetened almond milk
- 1/2 tsp cinnamon
- Ice cubes (optional)

Directions:

1. Put the entire components inside a mixer.

2. Blend till smooth.

3. Place ice cubes if you prefer a colder smoothie.

4. Pour into a glass and relish!

Per serving: Calories: 320kcal; Fat: 20g; Carbs: 30g; Protein: 8g

20. Veggie and Tofu Scramble

Preparation time: 10 mins

Cooking time: 10 mins

Servings: 2

Ingredients:

- 1/2 block firm tofu, crumbled
- 1/2 teacup cubed bell peppers
- 1/2 teacup cubed onions
- 1/2 teacup cubed tomatoes
- 1/2 teacup fresh spinach leaves
- Salt and pepper as required
- Small amount of olive oil

Directions:

1. Warm your non-stick griddle inside a middling temp. then lightly coat it using olive oil.

2. Include cubed onions and bell peppers then sauté for 2-3 mins.

3. Stir in cubed tomatoes and crumbled tofu.

4. Cook for an extra 5-7 mins, stirring occasionally.

5. Include fresh spinach leaves then cook till wilted.

6. Season using salt and pepper and serve hot.

Per serving: Calories: 180kcal; Fat: 10g; Carbs: 14g; Protein: 14g

21. Mediterranean Scrambled Eggs

Preparation time: 5 mins

Cooking time: 5 mins

Servings: 2

Ingredients:

- 4 big eggs
- 1/2 teacup cubed tomatoes
- 1/4 teacup cubed cucumber
- 1/4 teacup cubed red onion
- 2 tbsps crumbled feta cheese
- Fresh parsley for garnish (optional)
- Salt and pepper as required
- Small amount of olive oil

Directions:

1. Warm your non-stick griddle inside a middling temp. then lightly coat it using olive oil.

2. Inside your container, whisk the eggs, season using salt and pepper.

3. Pour the eggs into your griddle and scramble till cooked.

4. Stir in cubed tomatoes, cucumber, and red onion.

5. Cook for an extra 2-3 mins, till the veggies are warmed.

6. Sprinkle crumbled feta cheese on top.

7. Garnish using fresh parsley if wanted.

8. Serve warm.

Per serving: Calories: 220kcal; Fat: 15g; Carbs: 6g; Protein: 15g

22. Peanut Butter Banana Oatmeal

Preparation time: 5 mins

Cooking time: 5 mins

Servings: 1

Ingredients:

- 1/2 teacup rolled oats
- 1 teacup unsweetened almond milk
- 1 ripe banana, mashed
- 2 tbsps natural peanut butter
- 1/2 tsp cinnamon
- 1 tbsp severed nuts (e.g., almonds, walnuts)

Directions:

1. Inside your saucepot, blend rolled oats and almond milk.

2. Cook inside a middling temp., stirring occasionally, 'til the oats are creamy then cooked through, around 5 mins.

3. Stir in mashed banana, peanut butter, and cinnamon.

4. Cook for an extra minute.

5. Transfer to a bowl and top with severed nuts.

6. Serve warm.

Per serving: Calories: 450kcal; Fat: 19g; Carbs: 60g; Protein: 13g

23. Spinach and Tomato Breakfast Wrap

Preparation time: 10 mins

Cooking time: 5 mins

Servings: 1

Ingredients:

- 1 whole-grain tortilla
- 2 big eggs
- 1/2 teacup fresh spinach leaves
- 1/2 teacup cubed tomatoes
- 2 tbsps shredded low-fat cheese
- Salt and pepper as required
- Small amount of olive oil

Directions:

1. Warm your non-stick griddle inside a middling temp. then lightly coat it using olive oil.

2. Scramble the eggs in the griddle 'til they are cooked to your liking.

3. Put your whole-grain tortilla on a plate.

4. Lay fresh spinach leaves on the tortilla.

5. Spoon the scrambled eggs on top.

6. Include cubed tomatoes and shredded cheese.

7. Season using salt and pepper.

8. Roll the tortilla, cut in half, and serve.

Per serving: Calories: 350kcal; Fat: 15g; Carbs: 30g; Protein: 23g

24. Berry Protein Smoothie

Preparation time: 5 mins

Servings: 1

Ingredients:

- 1 teacup unsweetened almond milk
- 1/2 teacup frozen mixed berries (e.g., strawberries, blueberries)
- 1 scoop of plant-based protein powder
- 1 tbsp chia seeds (optional)
- Ice cubes (optional)

Directions:

1. Put the entire components inside a mixer.

2. Blend till smooth and creamy.

3. Place ice cubes if you prefer a colder smoothie.

4. Pour into a glass and relish!

Per serving: Calories: 250kcal; Fat: 9g; Carbs: 20g; Protein: 25g

25. Turkey and Spinach Breakfast Burrito

Preparation time: 10 mins

Cooking time: 5 mins

Servings: 2

Ingredients:

- 4 big eggs
- 1/2 teacup cubed turkey breast (cooked)
- 1/2 teacup fresh spinach leaves
- 2 whole-grain tortillas
- Salt and pepper as required
- Small amount of olive oil

Directions:

1. Inside your container, whisk the eggs and season using salt and pepper.

2. Warm your non-stick griddle inside a middling temp. then lightly coat it using olive oil.

3. Bring the whisked eggs into your griddle and scramble till cooked.

4. Stir in cubed turkey breast and fresh spinach leaves till the spinach wilts.

5. Split your egg mixture between the two tortillas.

6. Roll each tortilla, folding in the sides, to create a burrito.

7. Serve warm.

Per serving: Calories: 320kcal; Fat: 12g; Carbs: 25g; Protein: 25g

Lunch Recipes

26. Grilled Lemon Herb Chicken

Preparation time: 10 mins

Cooking time: 15 mins

Servings: 4

Ingredients:

- 4 boneless, skinless chicken breasts
- 2 lemons
- 2 tbsps olive oil
- 2 pieces garlic, crushed
- 1 tsp dried oregano
- Salt and pepper as required

Directions:

1. Warm up your grill or stovetop grill pan inside a med-high temp.

2. Inside your container, blend the juice of one lemon, olive oil, crushed garlic, dried oregano, salt, and pepper to form a marinade.

3. Put your chicken breasts in your resealable plastic bag or your shallow dish then pour your marinade across them. Seal or cover and let them marinate for almost 10 mins.

4. Grill the chicken for around 6-7 mins on all sides, or 'til it's cooked through and has nice grill marks.

5. While grilling, slice the remaining lemon into wedges to serve alongside the chicken.

6. Once done, serve the grilled chicken with lemon wedges for an extra burst of flavor.

Per serving: Calories: 180kcal; Fat: 7g; Carbs: 3g; Protein: 26g

27. Baked Chicken and Vegetable Packets

Preparation time: 15 mins

Cooking time: 30 mins

Servings: 4

Ingredients:

- 4 boneless, skinless chicken breasts
- 2 teacups mixed vegetables (e.g., carrots, bell peppers, zucchini), severed
- 2 tbsps olive oil
- 2 pieces garlic, crushed
- 1 tsp dried thyme
- Salt and pepper as required

Directions:

1. Warm up your oven to 375 deg.F.

2. Lay out 4 big squares of your aluminum foil.

3. Put your chicken breast in the center of each foil square.

4. Split the severed vegetables uniformly among the packets, organizing them around the chicken.

5. Inside your small container, whisk collectively olive oil, crushed garlic, dried thyme, salt, and pepper.

6. Spray the garlic thyme mixture over each chicken breast and vegetables.

7. Fold and seal the foil packets tightly.

8. Bake for 25-30 mins or 'til the chicken is cooked through then the vegetables are soft.

Per serving: Calories: 250kcal; Fat: 10g; Carbs: 7g; Protein: 30g

28. Mediterranean Chickpea Salad

Preparation time: 15 mins

Cooking time: 0 mins

Servings: 4

Ingredients:

• 2 cans (15 oz. each) chickpeas, that is drained and washed

• 1 cucumber, cubed

• 1 teacup cherry tomatoes, divided

• 1/2 red onion, finely severed

• 1/4 teacup fresh parsley, severed

• Juice of 2 lemons

• 2 tbsps olive oil

• 1 tsp dried oregano

• Salt and pepper as required

Directions:

1. Inside your big container, blend chickpeas, cucumber, cherry tomatoes, red onion, and fresh parsley.

2. Inside your distinct container, whisk collectively lemon juice, salt, olive oil, dried oregano, and pepper to create the dressing.

3. Transfer the dressing over the salad and toss to blend.

4. Chill the Mediterranean chickpea salad in your refrigerator for almost 30 mins prior to serving.

Per serving: Calories: 290kcal; Fat: 10g; Carbs: 40g; Protein: 10g

29. Grilled Herb-Marinated Turkey Breast

Preparation time: 10 mins

Cooking time: 20 mins

Servings: 4

Ingredients:

• 4 boneless, skinless turkey breast fillets

• 2 tbsps olive oil

• 2 pieces garlic, crushed

• 1 tbsp fresh rosemary, severed

• 1 tbsp fresh thyme, severed

• Salt and pepper as required

• Lemon wedges for serving (optional)

Directions:

1. Inside your container, blend olive oil, crushed garlic, fresh rosemary, fresh thyme, salt, and pepper to form a marinade.

2. Coat the turkey breast fillets using the marinade and let them sit for almost 10 mins.

3. Warm up your grill to med-high temp.

4. Grill the turkey breasts for around 8-10 mins on all sides, or 'til they are cooked through and have grill marks.

5. Serve with lemon wedges if wanted.

Per serving: Calories: 220kcal; Fat: 7g; Carbs: 1g; Protein: 36g

30. Lemon Garlic Grilled Tofu

Preparation time: 15 mins

Cooking time: 10 mins

Servings: 4

Ingredients:

- 1 block extra-firm tofu, sliced into rectangles
- Juice of 2 lemons
- 2 pieces garlic, crushed
- 2 tbsps olive oil
- 1 tsp dried thyme
- Salt and pepper as required

Directions:

1. Inside your container, blend the juice of two lemons, crushed garlic, olive oil, dried thyme, salt, and pepper to form a marinade.

2. Put your tofu slices in your resealable plastic bag or your shallow dish then pour the marinade across them. Seal or cover and let them marinate for almost 10 mins.

3. Warm up your grill or stovetop grill pan inside a med-high temp.

4. Grill the tofu for around 4-5 mins on all sides, or 'til it's nicely grilled and mildly crispy.

5. Serve warm.

Per serving: Calories: 190kcal; Fat: 14g; Carbs: 6g; Protein: 13g

31. Sautéed Spinach and Mushroom Chicken

Preparation time: 10 mins

Cooking time: 20 mins

Servings: 4

Ingredients:

- 4 boneless, skinless chicken breasts
- 8 oz. mushrooms, sliced
- 4 teacups fresh spinach
- 2 pieces garlic, crushed
- 2 tbsps olive oil
- Juice of 1 lemon
- Salt and pepper as required

Directions:

1. Season chicken breasts with salt and pepper.

2. Warm olive oil in your big skillet inside a med-high temp.

3. Include chicken breasts then cook for around 5-6 mins on all sides, or 'til they are cooked through.

4. Take out the chicken from your griddle then put away.

5. Inside your similar griddle, include crushed garlic and sliced mushrooms. Sauté for around 5 mins till the mushrooms are browned.

6. Include fresh spinach to your griddle then cook till it wilts, about 2-3 mins.

7. Return the cooked chicken to your griddle, drizzle with lemon juice, and heat through.

8. Serve warm.

Per serving: Calories: 250kcal; Fat: 10g; Carbs: 5g; Protein: 32g

32. Spinach and Feta Stuffed Chicken Breasts

Preparation time: 20 mins

Cooking time: 30 mins

Servings: 4

Ingredients:

- 4 boneless, skinless chicken breasts
- 2 teacups fresh spinach
- 1/2 teacup crumbled feta cheese (low-fat if preferred)
- 2 pieces garlic, crushed
- 1 tbsp olive oil
- Salt and pepper as required
- Toothpicks

Directions:

1. Warm up your oven to 375 deg.F.

2. Inside your griddle, warm olive oil inside a med-high temp.

3. Include crushed garlic then sauté for around 30 secs till fragrant.

4. Include fresh spinach then cook till wilted.

5. Take out from heat then stir in crumbled feta cheese.

6. Cut a horizontal slit along the thickest part of each of your chicken breast to create a pocket.

7. Stuff each pocket using the spinach and feta mixture and secure with toothpicks.

8. Season the stuffed chicken breasts with salt and pepper.

9. Bake in the oven for 25-30 mins, or 'til the chicken is cooked through.

10. Take out toothpicks prior to serving.

Per serving: Calories: 250kcal; Fat: 10g; Carbs: 2g; Protein: 36g

33. Lemon Herb Baked Cod

Preparation time: 10 mins

Cooking time: 15 mins

Servings: 4

Ingredients:

- 4 cod fillets
- Juice of 2 lemons
- 2 tbsps olive oil
- 2 pieces garlic, crushed
- 1 tsp dried basil
- Salt and pepper as required
- Fresh parsley for garnish (optional)

Directions:

1. Warm up your oven to 375 deg.F.

2. Put your cod fillets on your baking sheet lined using parchment paper.

3. Inside your container, blend the juice of two lemons, olive oil, crushed garlic, dried basil, salt, and pepper to form a marinade.

4. Spray the marinade over the cod fillets.

5. Bake for 12-15 mins or 'til the cod flakes easily using a fork.

6. Garnish using fresh parsley if wanted prior to serving.**Per serving:** Calories: 180kcal; Fat: 7g; Carbs: 3g; Protein: 25g

34. Quinoa Stuffed Bell Peppers

Preparation time: 20 mins

Cooking time: 30 mins

Servings: 4

Ingredients:

- 4 bell peppers, any color

- 1 teacup quinoa
- 2 teacups vegetable broth (low-sodium)
- 1 can (15 oz) black beans, that is drained & washed
- 1 teacup cubed tomatoes
- 1 tsp chili powder
- 1 teacup corn kernels
- Salt and pepper as required
- Fresh cilantro for garnish (optional)

Directions:

1. Warm up your oven to 375 deg.F.

2. Cut your tops off the bell peppers and take out the seeds and membranes. Put away.

3. Inside your saucepot, raise vegetable broth to a boil. Include quinoa, decrease temp. to low, cover, then simmer for around 15 mins, or 'til quinoa is cooked and liquid is engrossed.

4. Inside your container, blend cooked quinoa, black beans, corn, cubed tomatoes, chili powder, salt, and pepper. Stuff each of your bell pepper with the quinoa mixture.

5. Put your stuffed bell peppers in your baking dish and cover with aluminum foil.

6. Bake for 20-25 mins or 'til the bell peppers are soft.

7. Garnish using fresh cilantro if wanted prior to serving.

Per serving: Calories: 280kcal; Fat: 3g; Carbs: 54g; Protein: 10g

35. Grilled Portobello Mushroom Steaks

Preparation time: 10 mins

Cooking time: 10 mins

Servings: 4

Ingredients:

- 4 big portobello mushroom caps
- 2 tbsps balsamic vinegar
- 2 tbsps olive oil
- 2 pieces garlic, crushed
- 1 tsp dried thyme
- Salt and pepper as required
- Fresh parsley for garnish (optional)

Directions:

1. Warm up your grill to med-high temp.

2. Inside your container, blend balsamic vinegar, olive oil, salt, crushed garlic, dried thyme, and pepper to form a marinade.

3. Brush the mushroom caps using the marinade on both sides.

4. Grill the mushroom caps for around 4-5 mins on all sides, or 'til they are soft and have grill marks.

5. Garnish using fresh parsley if wanted prior to serving.

Per serving: Calories: 100kcal; Fat: 7g; Carbs: 6g; Protein: 4g

36. Spaghetti Squash with Tomato Basil Sauce

Preparation time: 10 mins

Cooking time: 45 mins

Servings: 4

Ingredients:

- 1 spaghetti squash
- 2 teacups tomato sauce (low-sodium)
- 1/4 teacup fresh basil, severed
- 2 pieces garlic, crushed
- 1 tbsp olive oil
- Salt and pepper as required
- Grated Parmesan cheese for garnish (optional)

Directions:

1. Warm up your oven to 375 deg.F.

2. Cut your spaghetti squash in half lengthwise and take out the seeds. Put your squash halves, cut side down, on your baking sheet then bake for around 40-45 mins, or 'til the flesh is soft.

3. While your squash is baking, warm olive oil in your saucepan inside a middling temp.

4. Include crushed garlic then sauté for around 30 secs till fragrant.

5. Pour in the tomato sauce and fresh basil. Season using salt and pepper. Simmer for 10 mins. Scrape the cooked spaghetti squash using a fork to create "noodles."

6. Serve the spaghetti squash with the tomato basil sauce and garnish using grated Parmesan cheese if wanted.

Per serving: Calories: 120kcal; Fat: 4g; Carbs: 20g; Protein: 3g

37. Grilled Lemon Dill Salmon

Preparation time: 10 mins

Cooking time: 15 mins

Servings: 4

Ingredients:

- 4 salmon fillets
- Juice of 2 lemons
- 2 tbsps olive oil
- 2 pieces garlic, crushed
- 1 tbsp fresh dill, severed
- Salt and pepper as required
- Lemon wedges for serving (optional)

Directions:

1. Warm up your grill to med-high temp.

2. Inside your container, blend the juice of two lemons, olive oil, crushed garlic, fresh dill, salt, and pepper to form a marinade.

3. Put your salmon fillets in your resealable plastic bag or your shallow dish then pour the marinade across them. Seal or cover and let them marinate for almost 10 mins.

4. Grill the salmon for around 5-7 mins on all sides, or 'til it flakes simply using a fork.

5. Serve with lemon wedges if wanted.

Per serving: Calories: 270kcal; Fat: 16g; Carbs: 2g; Protein: 29g

38. Baked Cod with Tomato and Olive Tapenade

Preparation time: 15 mins

Cooking time: 15 mins

Servings: 4

Ingredients:

• 4 cod fillets

• 1 teacup cherry tomatoes, divided

• 1/4 teacup kalamata olives, that is pitted and sliced

• 2 tbsps olive oil

• 2 pieces garlic, crushed

• 1 tbsp capers (optional)

• Salt and pepper as required

• Fresh parsley for garnish (optional)

Directions:

1. Warm up your oven to 375 deg.F.

2. Inside your container, blend cherry tomatoes, sliced kalamata olives, crushed garlic, capers (if using), olive oil, salt, and pepper to create the tapenade.

3. Put your cod fillets in your baking dish and spoon the tapenade across them.

4. Bake for 15-20 mins or 'til the cod flakes easily using a fork and the tomatoes have softened.

5. Garnish using fresh parsley if wanted prior to serving.

Per serving: Calories: 220kcal; Fat: 10g; Carbs: 6g; Protein: 27g

39. Quinoa and Chickpea Salad

Preparation time: 20 mins

Cooking time: 15 mins

Servings: 4

Ingredients:

• 1 teacup quinoa

• 2 teacups vegetable broth (low-sodium)

• 1 can (15 oz.) chickpeas, that is drained and washed

• 1 cucumber, cubed

• 1 red bell pepper, cubed

• 1/4 teacup fresh parsley, severed

• Juice of 1 lemon

• 2 tbsps olive oil

• Salt and pepper as required

Directions:

1. Inside your saucepot, bring vegetable broth to a boil. Include quinoa, decrease temp. to low, cover, then simmer for around 15 mins, or 'til quinoa is cooked and liquid is engrossed. Fluff using a fork and let it cool.

2. Inside your big container, blend cooked quinoa, chickpeas, cubed cucumber, cubed red bell pepper, and severed fresh parsley.

3. Inside your distinct small container, whisk collectively the juice of one lemon, salt, olive oil, and pepper to create the dressing.

4. Transfer the dressing over the salad and toss to blend.

5. Serve the quinoa and chickpea salad.

Per serving: Calories: 300kcal; Fat: 10g; Carbs: 45g; Protein: 10g

40. Balsamic Glazed Chicken with Roasted Vegetables

Preparation time: 20 mins

Cooking time: 30 mins

Servings: 4

Ingredients:

- 4 boneless, skinless chicken breasts
- 2 teacups mixed vegetables (e.g., carrots, broccoli, cauliflower), severed
- 1/4 teacup balsamic vinegar
- 2 tbsps olive oil
- 2 tbsps honey
- 2 pieces garlic, crushed
- Salt and pepper as required
- Fresh thyme for garnish (optional)

Directions:

1. Warm up your oven to 400 deg.F.

2. Inside your container, whisk collectively balsamic vinegar, olive oil, honey, crushed garlic, salt, and pepper to create the glaze.

3. Place chicken breasts and severed vegetables on your baking sheet.

4. Brush the chicken and vegetables with the balsamic glaze.

5. Roast in the oven for 25-30 mins, or 'til the chicken is cooked through and the vegetables are soft.

6. Garnish using fresh thyme if wanted prior to serving.

Per serving: Calories: 300kcal; Fat: 10g; Carbs: 24g; Protein: 30g

41. Shrimp and Asparagus Stir-Fry

Preparation time: 15 mins

Cooking time: 10 mins

Servings: 4

Ingredients:

- 1 lb. large shrimp, skinned and deveined
- 2 bunches asparagus, that is clipped then cut into 2-inch pieces
- 1 red bell pepper, finely cut
- 2 pieces garlic, crushed
- 2 tbsps low-sodium soy sauce
- 1 tbsp olive oil
- 1 tsp ginger, grated
- Salt and pepper as required
- Sliced green onions for garnish (optional)

Directions:

1. Warm olive oil in your big griddle or wok inside a med-high temp.

2. Include crushed garlic and grated ginger then sauté for around 30 secs till fragrant.

3. Include shrimp to your griddle then cook for around 2-3 mins on all sides 'til they turn pink and opaque. Take out them from the griddle and put away.

4. Inside your similar griddle, include asparagus and red bell pepper. Stir-fry for around 4-5 mins till the vegetables are soft-crisp.

5. Return the cooked shrimp to your griddle, include low-sodium soy sauce, and stir to blend.

6. Season using salt and pepper.

7. Garnish using sliced green onions if wanted prior to serving.

Per serving: Calories: 180kcal; Fat: 4g; Carbs: 8g; Protein: 25g

42. Greek-inspired Quinoa Salad

Preparation time: 20 mins

Cooking time: 15 mins

Servings: 4

Ingredients:

- 1 teacup quinoa
- 2 teacups vegetable broth (low-sodium)
- 1 cucumber, cubed
- 1 teacup cherry tomatoes, divided
- 1/2 red onion, finely severed
- 1/4 teacup kalamata olives, that is pitted and sliced
- 1/4 teacup crumbled feta cheese (low-fat if preferred)
- Juice of 1 lemon
- 2 tbsps olive oil
- 1 tsp dried oregano
- Salt and pepper as required

Directions:

1. Inside your saucepot, bring vegetable broth to a boil. Include quinoa, decrease temp. to low, cover, then simmer for around 15 mins, or 'til quinoa is cooked and liquid is engrossed. Fluff using a fork and let it cool.

2. Inside your big container, blend cooked quinoa, cubed cucumber, divided cherry tomatoes, finely severed red onion, sliced kalamata olives, and crumbled feta cheese.

3. Inside your distinct small container, whisk collectively the juice of one lemon, olive oil, dried oregano, salt, and pepper to create the dressing. Transfer the dressing over the salad and toss to blend.

4. Serve the Greek-inspired quinoa salad.

Per serving: Calories: 320kcal; Fat: 13g; Carbs: 44g; Protein: 9g

43. Stir-Fried Tofu and Broccoli

Preparation time: 15 mins

Cooking time: 15 mins

Servings: 4

Ingredients:

- 1 block extra-firm tofu, cubed
- 4 teacups broccoli florets
- 2 pieces garlic, crushed
- 2 tbsps low-sodium soy sauce
- 1 tbsp olive oil
- Salt and pepper as required
- Sliced green onions for garnish (optional)

Directions:

1. Press tofu to take out excess moisture then cut it into cubes.

2. Warm olive oil in your big griddle or wok inside a med-high temp.

3. Include cubed tofu then cook till golden brown on all sides. Take out from the griddle and put away.

4. Inside your similar griddle, include crushed garlic then sauté for around 30 secs.

5. Include broccoli florets and stir-fry for around 5-7 mins 'til they are soft-crisp.

6. Return the cooked tofu to your griddle, include low-sodium soy sauce, and stir to blend.

7. Season using salt and pepper.

8. Garnish using sliced green onions if wanted prior to serving.

Per serving: Calories: 160kcal; Fat: 9g; Carbs: 11g; Protein: 13g

44. Thai-inspired Tofu and Vegetable Stir-Fry

Preparation time: 20 mins

Cooking time: 15 mins

Servings: 4

Ingredients:

- 1 block extra-firm tofu, cubed
- 2 teacups mixed vegetables (e.g., broccoli, bell peppers, snap peas), severed
- 1/4 teacup low-sodium soy sauce
- 2 tbsps olive oil
- 2 pieces garlic, crushed
- 1 tbsp fresh ginger, crushed
- 1 tbsp honey
- Salt and pepper as required
- Chopped cilantro for garnish (optional)

Directions:

1. Press tofu to take out excess moisture then cut it into cubes.

2. Inside your container, whisk collectively low-sodium soy sauce, crushed garlic, crushed ginger, honey, salt, and pepper to create a stir-fry sauce.

3. Warm olive oil in your big griddle or wok inside a med-high temp.

4. Include cubed tofu and stir-fry for around 5-7 mins till golden brown. Take out from the griddle and put away.

5. Inside your similar griddle, include mixed vegetables and stir-fry for around 5 mins 'til they are soft-crisp.

6. Return the cooked tofu to your griddle, include the stir-fry sauce, and stir to blend.

7. Cook for an extra 2-3 mins.

8. Garnish using severed cilantro if wanted prior to serving.

Per serving: Calories: 220kcal; Fat: 11g; Carbs: 15g; Protein: 16g

45. Teriyaki Tofu Stir-Fry

Preparation time: 20 mins

Cooking time: 15 mins

Servings: 4

Ingredients:

- 1 block extra-firm tofu, cubed
- 2 teacups mixed vegetables (e.g., broccoli, carrots, bell peppers), severed
- 1/4 teacup low-sodium teriyaki sauce
- 2 tbsps olive oil
- 2 pieces garlic, crushed
- 1 tsp ginger, crushed
- Salt and pepper as required
- Sesame seeds for garnish (optional)

Directions:

1. Press tofu to take out excess moisture then cut it into cubes.

2. Inside your container, whisk collectively low-sodium teriyaki sauce, crushed garlic, crushed ginger, salt, and pepper.

3. Warm olive oil in your big griddle or wok inside a med-high temp.

4. Include cubed tofu and stir-fry for around 5-7 mins till golden brown. Take out from the griddle and put away.

5. Inside your similar griddle, include mixed vegetables and stir-fry for around 5 mins 'til they are soft-crisp.

6. Return the cooked tofu to your griddle, include the teriyaki sauce mixture, and stir to blend.

7. Cook for an extra 2-3 mins.

8. Garnish using sesame seeds if wanted prior to serving.

Per serving: Calories: 250kcal; Fat: 12g; Carbs: 20g; Protein: 16g

46. Baked Eggplant Parmesan

Preparation time: 20 mins

Cooking time: 35 mins

Servings: 4

Ingredients:

- 2 big eggplants, sliced into rounds
- 2 teacups marinara sauce (low-sodium)
- 1 teacup part-skim mozzarella cheese, shredded
- 1/2 teacup grated Parmesan cheese
- 1/4 teacup fresh basil leaves, severed
- 2 tbsps olive oil
- Salt and pepper as required

Directions:

1. Warm up your oven to 375 deg.F.

2. Brush eggplant slices using olive oil and season using salt and pepper.

3. Put your eggplant slices on your baking sheet then bake for around 15-20 mins, or 'til they are soft.

4. In a baking dish, layer half of the marinara sauce, followed by half of the eggplant slices, half of the mozzarella cheese, and half of the Parmesan cheese. Repeat the layers.

5. Bake for an extra 15 mins, or 'til the cheese is bubbly and golden.

6. Take out from the oven and garnish using severed fresh basil.

7. Serve the baked eggplant Parmesan.

Per serving: Calories: 280kcal; Fat: 15g; Carbs: 27g; Protein: 12g

47. Lemon Garlic Shrimp and Zucchini Noodles

Preparation time: 15 mins

Cooking time: 10 mins

Servings: 4

Ingredients:

- 1 lb. large shrimp, skinned and deveined
- 4 medium zucchinis, spiralized into noodles
- 2 pieces garlic, crushed
- Juice of 2 lemons
- 2 tbsps olive oil
- 1 tbsp fresh parsley, severed
- Salt and pepper as required
- Lemon wedges for garnish (optional)

Directions:

1. Inside your container, blend the lemon juice, olive oil, crushed garlic, fresh parsley, salt, and pepper to form a marinade.

2. Put your shrimp in your resealable plastic bag or your shallow dish then pour the marinade across them. Seal or cover and let them marinate for around 10 mins.

3. Heat a big griddle inside a med-high temp.

4. Include the marinated shrimp then cook for around 2-3 mins on all sides 'til they turn pink and opaque. Take out them from the griddle and put away. Inside your similar griddle, include zucchini noodles and stir-fry for around 3-4 mins 'til they are soft-crisp.

5. Return the cooked shrimp to your griddle and toss to blend. Serve with lemon wedges if wanted.

Per serving: Calories: 180kcal; Fat: 7g; Carbs: 10g; Protein: 20g

48. Stuffed Bell Peppers with Ground Turkey

Preparation time: 20 mins

Cooking time: 45 mins

Servings: 4

Ingredients:

- 4 bell peppers, any color
- 1 lb. lean ground turkey
- 1 teacup cooked brown rice
- 1 can (14 oz.) cubed tomatoes (low-sodium)
- 1/2 onion, severed
- 2 pieces garlic, crushed
- 2 tbsps olive oil
- 1 tsp Italian seasoning
- Salt and pepper as required

Directions:

1. Warm up your oven to 375 deg.F.

2. Cut your tops off the bell peppers and take out the seeds and membranes. Put away.

3. Inside your griddle, cook lean ground turkey inside a middling temp. till browned. Drain any excess fat.

4. Bring your severed onion and crushed garlic to your griddle then sauté for around 3-4 mins 'til they are softened.

5. Stir in cooked brown rice, cubed tomatoes (with their juice), Italian seasoning, salt, and pepper. Mix well.

6. Stuff each bell pepper with the ground turkey and rice mixture.

7. Bring your stuffed bell peppers in your baking dish and cover with aluminum foil.

8. Bake for 35-40 mins or 'til the bell peppers are soft.

9. Serve the stuffed bell peppers hot.

Per serving: Calories: 280kcal; Fat: 10g; Carbs: 26g; Protein: 23g

49. Chicken and Broccoli Stir-Fry

Preparation time: 15 mins

Cooking time: 15 mins

Servings: 4

Ingredients:

- 4 boneless, skinless chicken breasts, that is cut into cubes
- 4 teacups broccoli florets
- 2 pieces garlic, crushed
- 1/4 teacup low-sodium soy sauce
- 2 tbsps olive oil
- 1 tbsp honey
- 1 tsp ginger, grated
- Salt and pepper as required
- Sesame seeds for garnish (optional)

Directions:

1. Inside your container, whisk collectively low-sodium soy sauce, honey, salt, grated ginger, crushed garlic, and pepper to create a stir-fry sauce.

2. Warm olive oil in your big griddle or wok inside a med-high temp.

3. Include chicken cubes and stir-fry for around 5-7 mins 'til they are cooked through.

4. Take out your cooked chicken from the griddle then put away.

5. Inside your similar griddle, include broccoli florets and stir-fry for around 4-5 mins 'til they are soft-crisp.

6. Return the cooked chicken to your griddle, include the stir-fry sauce, and toss to blend.

7. Cook for an extra 2-3 mins.

8. Garnish using sesame seeds if wanted prior to serving.

Per serving: Calories: 260kcal; Fat: 9g; Carbs: 15g; Protein: 29g

50. Turkey and Vegetable Skillet

Preparation time: 15 mins

Cooking time: 20 mins

Servings: 4

Ingredients:

- 1 lb. lean ground turkey
- 2 teacups mixed vegetables (e.g., broccoli, carrots, bell peppers), severed
- 1 onion, severed
- 2 pieces garlic, crushed
- 2 tbsps olive oil
- 1 tsp dried Italian seasoning
- Salt and pepper as required
- Fresh parsley for garnish (optional)

Directions:

1. Warm olive oil in your big griddle inside a med-high temp.

2. Include your severed onion and crushed garlic then sauté for around 3-4 mins 'til they are softened.

3. Include lean ground turkey then cook till browned, breaking it apart with a spatula.

4. Stir in mixed vegetables then cook for 5-7 mins 'til they are soft.

5. Season with dried Italian seasoning, salt, and pepper.

6. Cook for an extra 2-3 mins, allowing the flavors to meld.

7. Garnish using fresh parsley if wanted prior to serving.

Per serving: Calories: 250kcal; Fat: 10g; Carbs: 12g; Protein: 28g

Dinner Recipes

51. Baked Turkey and Vegetable Foil Packets

Preparation time: 15 mins

Cooking time: 30 mins

Servings: 4

Ingredients:

- 1 lb. lean ground turkey
- 2 teacups mixed vegetables (e.g., bell peppers, zucchini, carrots), severed
- 2 tbsps olive oil
- 2 pieces garlic, crushed
- 1 tsp Italian seasoning
- Salt and pepper as required
- Fresh parsley for garnish (optional)

Directions:

1. Warm up your oven to 375 deg.F.

2. Inside your big container, blend lean ground turkey, mixed vegetables, olive oil, crushed garlic, Italian seasoning, salt, and pepper.

3. Tear four large squares of aluminum foil.

4. Split the turkey and vegetable mixture uniformly among the foil squares.

5. Fold and seal the foil packets tightly.

6. Put your packets on your baking sheet then bake for 25-30 mins, or 'til the turkey is cooked through and the vegetables are soft.

7. Garnish using fresh parsley if wanted prior to serving.

Per serving: Calories: 220kcal; Fat: 12g; Carbs: 9g; Protein: 19g

52. Zucchini Noodles with Pesto

Preparation time: 15 mins

Cooking time: 5 mins

Servings: 4

Ingredients:

- 4 medium zucchinis, spiralized into noodles
- 1 teacup cherry tomatoes, divided
- 1/4 teacup pesto sauce (homemade or store-bought, preferably low-fat)
- 2 tbsps grated Parmesan cheese (optional)
- Salt and pepper as required
- Fresh basil leaves for garnish (optional)

Directions:

1. Warm a big griddle inside a med-high temp.

2. Include spiralized zucchini noodles then cook for around 2-3 mins 'til they are soft-crisp.

3. Stir in cherry tomato halves then cook for an extra 1-2 mins.

4. Take out from heat then toss the zucchini noodles and tomatoes with pesto sauce.

5. Season using salt and pepper.

6. Garnish using grated Parmesan cheese and fresh basil leaves if wanted prior to serving.

Per serving: Calories: 150kcal; Fat: 11g; Carbs: 9g; Protein: 5g

53. Grilled Vegetable Fajitas

Preparation time: 15 mins

Cooking time: 15 mins

Servings: 4

Ingredients:

- 2 bell peppers (any color), finely cut
- 1 red onion, finely cut
- 2 zucchinis, finely cut
- 2 tbsps olive oil
- 1 tbsp chili powder
- 1 tsp cumin
- Salt and pepper as required
- 8 small whole-wheat tortillas
- Salsa and sliced avocado (optional, for serving)

Directions:

1. Warm up your grill or stovetop grill pan inside a med-high temp.

2. Inside your big container, toss the sliced bell peppers, red onion, and zucchini using olive oil, chili powder, cumin, salt, and pepper.

3. Grill the vegetables for around 5-7 mins 'til they are soft and have grill marks.

4. Warm the whole-wheat tortillas on the grill for around 30 secs on all sides.

5. Serve the grilled vegetables in the tortillas, and top with salsa and sliced avocado if wanted.

Per serving: Calories: 280kcal; Fat: 8g; Carbs: 45g; Protein: 8g

54. Baked Salmon with Asparagus

Preparation time: 10 mins

Cooking time: 20 mins

Servings: 4

Ingredients:

- 4 salmon fillets
- 1 bunch asparagus spears
- 2 tbsps olive oil
- 1 lemon, finely cut
- Salt and pepper as required
- Fresh dill (optional)

Directions:

1. Warm up your oven to 375 deg.F.

2. Put your salmon fillets on your baking sheet lined using parchment paper.

3. Arrange the asparagus spears around the salmon.

4. Spray olive oil over the salmon and asparagus, then season using salt and pepper.

5. Place lemon slices on top of each salmon fillet.

6. Bake for 15-20 mins, or 'til the salmon flakes easily using a fork and the asparagus is soft.

7. Garnish using fresh dill if wanted prior to serving.

Per serving: Calories: 260kcal; Fat: 15g; Carbs: 6g; Protein: 26g

55. Seared Mahi-Mahi with Lemon Herb Sauce

Preparation time: 10 mins

Cooking time: 10 mins

Servings: 4

Ingredients:

- 4 mahi-mahi fillets
- Juice of 2 lemons
- 2 tbsps olive oil
- 2 pieces garlic, crushed
- 1 tbsp fresh parsley, severed
- 1 tbsp fresh dill, severed
- Salt and pepper as required

Directions:

1. Season mahi-mahi fillets with salt and pepper.

2. Warm olive oil in your big griddle inside a med-high temp.

3. Include mahi-mahi fillets and sear for around 3-4 mins on all sides, or 'til they are cooked through and have a golden crust.

4. Take out the mahi-mahi from the griddle and put away.

5. Inside your similar griddle, include crushed garlic then cook for around 30 secs till fragrant.

6. Stir in lemon juice, fresh parsley, and fresh dill. Cook for an extra minute.

7. Pour the lemon herb sauce over the mahi-mahi fillets and serve.

Per serving: Calories: 200kcal; Fat: 8g; Carbs: 3g; Protein: 29g

56. Grilled Herb-Marinated Portobello Mushrooms

Preparation time: 15 mins

Cooking time: 10 mins

Servings: 4

Ingredients:

- 4 big portobello mushroom caps
- 2 tbsps olive oil
- 2 pieces garlic, crushed
- 1 tbsp fresh herbs (e.g., rosemary, thyme, oregano), severed
- Salt and pepper as required
- Balsamic vinegar for drizzling (optional)

Directions:

1. Warm up your grill to med-high temp.

2. Inside your container, blend olive oil, crushed garlic, fresh herbs, salt, and pepper to form a marinade.

3. Brush both sides of the mushroom caps using the marinade.

4. Grill the mushrooms for around 4-5 mins on all sides 'til they are soft and have grill marks.

5. Spray with balsamic vinegar if wanted prior to serving.

Per serving: Calories: 80kcal; Fat: 7g; Carbs: 4g; Protein: 2g

57. Mushroom and Spinach Quinoa Bowl

Preparation time: 15 mins

Cooking time: 20 mins

Servings: 4

Ingredients:

• 1 teacup quinoa

• 2 teacups vegetable broth (low-sodium)

• 8 oz mushrooms, sliced

• 4 teacups fresh spinach

• 1 onion, severed

• 2 pieces garlic, crushed

• 2 tbsps olive oil

• 1 tsp dried thyme

• Salt and pepper as required

• Grated Parmesan cheese for topping (optional)

Directions:

1. Inside your saucepot, bring vegetable broth to a boil. Include quinoa, decrease temp. to low, cover, then simmer for around 15-20 mins, or 'til quinoa is cooked and liquid is engrossed. Fluff using a fork and let it cool.

2. While your quinoa is cooking, warm olive oil inside a griddle inside a med-high temp.

3. Bring your severed onion and crushed garlic to your griddle then sauté for around 3-4 mins 'til they are softened.

4. Stir in sliced mushrooms and dried thyme. Cook for around 5-7 mins till the mushrooms are soft and browned.

5. Include fresh spinach to your griddle then cook till wilted.

6. Blend the cooked quinoa with the mushroom and spinach mixture.

7. Season using salt and pepper.

8. Top with grated Parmesan cheese if wanted prior to serving.

Per serving: Calories: 270kcal; Fat: 8g; Carbs: 41g; Protein: 10g

58. Eggplant and Chickpea Curry

Preparation time: 15 mins

Cooking time: 25 mins

Servings: 4

Ingredients:

• 1 big eggplant, cubed

• 1 can (15 oz.) chickpeas, that is drained and washed

• 1 onion, severed

• 2 pieces garlic, crushed

• 1 can (14 oz.) cubed tomatoes

• 1 can (14 oz.) coconut milk (light version if preferred)

• 2 tbsps curry powder

• 1 tbsp olive oil

• Salt and pepper as required

• Fresh cilantro for garnish (optional)

Directions:

1. Warm olive oil in your big griddle inside a middling temp.

2. Include your severed onion and garlic then sauté for around 3-4 mins 'til they are softened.

3. Include curry powder then cook for an extra min to toast the spices.

4. Stir in eggplant cubes, chickpeas, cubed tomatoes, and coconut milk.

5. Season using salt and pepper. Stir to blend.

6. Cover the griddle and let it simmer for around 20 mins, or 'til the eggplant is soft.

7. Garnish using fresh cilantro if wanted and serve hot.

Per serving: Calories: 320kcal; Fat: 15g; Carbs: 40g; Protein: 9g

59. Lemon Herb Grilled Chicken Breasts

Preparation time: 10 mins

Cooking time: 15 mins

Servings: 4

Ingredients:

- 4 boneless, skinless chicken breasts
- 2 lemons
- 2 tbsps olive oil
- 2 pieces garlic, crushed
- 1 tsp dried thyme
- Salt and pepper as required
- Fresh basil for garnish (optional)

Directions:

1. Warm up your grill to med-high temp.

2. Inside your container, blend the juice of one lemon, olive oil, crushed garlic, dried thyme, salt, and pepper to form a marinade.

3. Put your chicken breasts in your resealable plastic bag or your shallow dish then pour the marinade across them. Seal or cover and let them marinate for almost 10 mins.

4. Grill the chicken for around 6-7 mins on all sides, or 'til they are cooked through and have nice grill marks.

5. While grilling, slice the remaining lemon into wedges to serve alongside the chicken.

6. Garnish using fresh basil if wanted prior to serving.

Per serving: Calories: 200kcal; Fat: 8g; Carbs: 2g; Protein: 30g

60. Broccoli and Chicken Stir-Fry

Preparation time: 15 mins

Cooking time: 15 mins

Servings: 4

Ingredients:

- 4 teacups broccoli florets
- 1 red bell pepper, finely cut
- 2 pieces garlic, crushed
- 2 tbsps low-sodium soy sauce
- 4 boneless, skinless chicken breasts, that is cut into strips
- 1 tbsp olive oil
- 1 tsp ginger, grated
- Salt and pepper as required
- Sliced green onions for garnish (optional)

Directions:

1. Warm olive oil in your big griddle or wok inside a med-high temp.

2. Include chicken strips then cook 'til they are browned then cooked through.

3. Take out the chicken from your skillet then put away.

4. Inside your similar griddle, include crushed garlic and grated ginger then sauté for around 30 secs.

5. Include broccoli florets and red bell pepper slices and stir-fry for around 5-7 mins till the vegetables are soft-crisp.

6. Return the cooked chicken to your griddle, include low-sodium soy sauce, and stir to blend.

7. Season using salt and pepper.

8. Garnish using sliced green onions if wanted prior to serving.

Per serving: Calories: 240kcal; Fat: 7g; Carbs: 10g; Protein: 30g

61. Black Bean and Veggie Tacos

Preparation time: 15 mins

Cooking time: 10 mins

Servings: 4 (2 tacos per serving)

Ingredients:

• 1 can (15 oz.) black beans, that is drained and washed

• 2 teacups mixed vegetables (e.g., bell peppers, onions, zucchini), severed

• 1 tbsp olive oil

• 1 tsp chili powder

• Salt and pepper as required

• 8 small whole wheat or corn tortillas

• Salsa and sliced avocado for topping (optional)

Directions:

1. Inside your griddle, warm olive oil inside a med-high temp.

2. Include your severed vegetables then sauté for around 5-7 mins 'til they are soft.

3. Stir in black beans, chili powder, salt, and pepper. Cook for an extra 2-3 mins to heat through.

4. Warm the tortillas in your dry skillet or microwave.

5. Spoon the black bean and veggie mixture into the tortillas.

6. Top with salsa and sliced avocado if wanted.

7. Serve the black bean and veggie tacos.

Per serving: Calories: 250kcal; Fat: 6g; Carbs: 43g; Protein: 9g

62. Quinoa and Black Bean Salad

Preparation time: 15 mins

Cooking time: 15 mins (for quinoa)

Servings: 4

Ingredients:

• 1 teacup quinoa

• 2 teacups water

• 1 can (15 oz.) black beans, that is drained and washed

• 1 teacup cherry tomatoes, divided

• 1/2 red onion, finely severed

• 1/4 teacup fresh cilantro, severed

• Juice of 2 limes

• 2 tbsps olive oil

• Salt and pepper as required

Directions:

1. Wash your quinoa under cold water and drain.

2. Inside your saucepot, place 2 teacups of water to a boil. Include quinoa, decrease temp. to low, cover, then simmer for around 15 mins, or 'til quinoa is soft and water is engrossed.

3. Fluff quinoa using a fork and let it cool to room temp.

4. Inside your big container, blend cooked quinoa, black beans, cherry tomatoes, red onion, and cilantro.

5. Inside your distinct container, whisk collectively lime juice, salt, olive oil, and pepper to create the dressing.

6. Transfer the dressing over the salad and toss to blend.

7. Chill the salad in your refrigerator for almost 30 mins prior to serving.

Per serving: Calories: 280kcal; Fat: 7g; Carbs: 47g; Protein: 9g

63. Lemon Garlic Roasted Chicken Thighs

Preparation time: 10 mins

Cooking time: 35 mins

Servings: 4

Ingredients:

- 4 bone-in, skin-on chicken thighs
- 2 lemons
- 2 tbsps olive oil
- 2 pieces garlic, crushed
- 1 tsp dried rosemary
- Salt and pepper as required
- Fresh rosemary sprigs for garnish (optional)

Directions:

1. Warm up your oven to 400 deg.F.

2. Inside your container, blend the juice of one lemon, olive oil, crushed garlic, dried rosemary, salt, and pepper to form a marinade.

3. Put your chicken thighs in your baking dish then pour the marinade across them.

4. Cut your other lemon into slices and arrange the slices around the chicken.

5. Roast the chicken thighs for around 30-35 mins, or 'til they are cooked through and the skin is crispy.

6. Garnish using fresh rosemary sprigs if wanted prior to serving.

Per serving: Calories: 320kcal; Fat: 21g; Carbs: 6g; Protein: 29g

64. Teriyaki Salmon with Stir-Fried Bok Choy

Preparation time: 15 mins

Cooking time: 15 mins

Servings: 4

Ingredients:

- 4 salmon fillets
- 4 baby bok choy, severed
- 1/4 teacup low-sodium teriyaki sauce
- 2 tbsps olive oil
- 2 pieces garlic, crushed
- 1 tsp ginger, grated
- Salt and pepper as required
- Sesame seeds for garnish (optional)

Directions:

1. Inside your container, blend low-sodium teriyaki sauce, crushed garlic, grated ginger, salt, and pepper.

2. Place salmon fillets in your resealable plastic bag or your shallow dish then pour the teriyaki marinade across them. Seal or cover and let them marinate for almost 10 mins.

3. Warm olive oil in your big griddle inside a med-high temp.

4. Take out salmon from the marinade then cook for around 3-4 mins on all sides 'til they are cooked through.

5. While your salmon is cooking, stir-fry the severed bok choy in the remaining marinade till it's soft-crisp.

6. Serve the teriyaki salmon alongside the stir-fried bok choy.

7. Garnish using sesame seeds if wanted prior to serving.

Per serving: Calories: 280kcal; Fat: 14g; Carbs: 10g; Protein: 28g

65. Turkey and Quinoa Stuffed Peppers

Preparation time: 20 mins

Cooking time: 40 mins

Servings: 4

Ingredients:

- 4 bell peppers, any color
- 1 lb. lean ground turkey
- 1 teacup cooked quinoa
- 1 can (14 oz.) cubed tomatoes, drained
- 1/2 onion, severed
- 2 pieces garlic, crushed
- 1 tsp Italian seasoning
- Salt and pepper as required

Directions:

1. Warm up your oven to 375 deg.F.

2. Cut your tops off the bell peppers and take out the seeds and membranes. Put away.

3. Inside your griddle, cook lean ground turkey inside a middling temp. till browned. Drain any excess fat.

4. Bring your severed onion and crushed garlic to your griddle then sauté for around 3-4 mins 'til they are softened.

5. Stir in cooked quinoa, cubed tomatoes, Italian seasoning, salt, and pepper. Mix well.

6. Stuff each of your bell pepper with the turkey and quinoa mixture.

7. Put your stuffed bell peppers in your baking dish and cover with aluminum foil.

8. Bake for 30-35 mins or 'til the bell peppers are soft.

9. Serve the turkey and quinoa stuffed peppers hot.

Per serving: Calories: 290kcal; Fat: 7g; Carbs: 32g; Protein: 26g

66. Greek Chicken and Vegetable Skewers

Preparation time: 20 mins

Cooking time: 15 mins

Servings: 4

Ingredients:

- 4 boneless, skinless chicken breasts, that is cut into cubes
- 2 bell peppers (any color), that is cut into chunks
- 1 red onion, that is cut into chunks
- Cherry tomatoes
- 1/4 teacup Greek yogurt (low-fat if preferred)
- Juice of 1 lemon
- 2 pieces garlic, crushed
- 1 tsp dried oregano
- Salt and pepper as required
- Wooden skewers, soaked in water

Directions:

1. Inside your container, blend Greek yogurt, lemon juice, salt, crushed garlic, dried oregano, and pepper to form a marinade.

2. Thread chicken, bell peppers, red onion, and cherry tomatoes onto the soaked wooden skewers.

3. Brush the skewers with the Greek yogurt marinade.

4. Warm up your grill to med-high temp.

5. Grill the skewers for around 10-15 mins, mixing irregularly, 'til the chicken is cooked through and the vegetables are soft.

6. Serve the Greek chicken and vegetable skewers.

Per serving: Calories: 240kcal; Fat: 5g; Carbs: 15g; Protein: 30g

67. Spaghetti Squash with Tomato and Basil Sauce

Preparation time: 15 mins

Cooking time: 45 mins

Servings: 4

Ingredients:

- 1 spaghetti squash
- 2 teacups tomato sauce (low-sodium)
- 1/4 teacup fresh basil leaves, severed
- 2 pieces garlic, crushed
- 2 tbsps olive oil
- Salt and pepper as required
- Grated Parmesan cheese for topping (optional)

Directions:

1. Warm up your oven to 375 deg.F.

2. Cut your spaghetti squash in half lengthwise then scoop out the seeds.

3. Put your squash halves, cut side down, on your baking sheet.

4. Bake for 30-40 mins, or 'til the squash flesh easily shreds into spaghetti-like strands using a fork.

5. While your squash is baking, warm olive oil in your saucepan inside a middling temp.

6. Include crushed garlic then sauté for around 30 secs till fragrant.

7. Stir in tomato sauce and severed basil. Simmer for around 10-15 mins.

8. Once the spaghetti squash is done, scrape the flesh into strands using a fork.

9. Serve the spaghetti squash topped with the tomato and basil sauce.

10. Garnish using grated Parmesan cheese if wanted.

Per serving: Calories: 150kcal; Fat: 7g; Carbs: 20g; Protein: 3g

68. Eggplant and Zucchini Ratatouille

Preparation time: 20 mins

Cooking time: 30 mins

Servings: 4

Ingredients:

- 1 eggplant, cubed
- 2 zucchinis, cubed
- 1 bell pepper, cubed
- 1 onion, severed
- 2 pieces garlic, crushed
- 1 can (14 oz) cubed tomatoes (low-sodium)
- 2 tbsps olive oil
- 1 tsp dried thyme
- Salt and pepper as required
- Fresh basil leaves for garnish (optional)

Directions:

1. Warm olive oil in your big griddle or pot inside a middling temp.

2. Include your severed onion and crushed garlic then sauté for around 3-4 mins 'til they are softened.

3. Include cubed eggplant, zucchini, and bell pepper to your griddle. Cook for 5-7 mins 'til they begin to soften.

4. Stir in cubed tomatoes (with their juice), dried thyme, salt, and pepper.

5. Cover then simmer for around 20 mins, stirring occasionally, 'til the vegetables are soft.

6. Garnish using fresh basil leaves if wanted prior to serving.

Per serving: Calories: 130kcal; Fat: 7g; Carbs: 16g; Protein: 3g

69. Greek Salad with Grilled Chicken

Preparation time: 15 mins

Cooking time: 15 mins

Servings: 4

Ingredients:

• 4 boneless, skinless chicken breasts

• 1 cucumber, cubed

• 1 teacup cherry tomatoes, divided

• 1/2 red onion, finely severed

• 1/4 teacup kalamata olives, that is pitted and sliced

• 1/4 teacup crumbled feta cheese (low-fat if preferred)

• Juice of 1 lemon

• 2 tbsps olive oil

• 1 tsp dried oregano

• Salt and pepper as required

Directions:

1. Season chicken breasts with dried oregano, salt, and pepper.
2. Warm up your grill to med-high temp.
3. Grill the chicken for around 6-7 mins on all sides, or 'til they are cooked through.
4. While grilling, prepare the salad by combining cubed cucumber, divided cherry tomatoes, finely severed red onion, sliced kalamata olives, and crumbled feta cheese inside a container.
5. Inside your distinct container, whisk collectively the juice of one lemon, salt, olive oil, and pepper to create the dressing.
6. Slice the grilled chicken then include it to the salad.
7. Transfer the dressing over the salad and chicken. Toss to blend.
8. Serve the Greek salad with grilled chicken.

Per serving: Calories: 320kcal; Fat: 15g; Carbs: 9g; Protein: 36g

70. Baked Cod with Lemon and Herbs

Preparation time: 15 mins

Cooking time: 20 mins

Servings: 4

Ingredients:

• 4 cod fillets

• Juice of 1 lemon

• 2 tbsps olive oil

• 2 pieces garlic, crushed

• 1 tbsp fresh herbs (e.g., dill, parsley, chives), severed

• Salt and pepper as required

• Lemon wedges for garnish (optional)

Directions:

1. Warm up your oven to 375 deg.F.

2. Inside your container, blend the juice of one lemon, olive oil, crushed garlic, fresh herbs, salt, and pepper.

3. Place cod fillets in your baking dish and drizzle them with the lemon and herb mixture.

4. Bake for around 15-20 mins, or 'til the cod flakes easily using a fork.

5. Serve the baked cod with lemon wedges if wanted.

Per serving: Calories: 220kcal; Fat: 8g; Carbs: 2g; Protein: 34g

71. Cauliflower Rice Stir-Fry with Tofu

Preparation time: 15 mins

Cooking time: 15 mins

Servings: 4

Ingredients:

- 1 block extra-firm tofu, cubed
- 4 teacups cauliflower rice (store-bought or homemade)
- 2 teacups mixed vegetables (e.g., broccoli, bell peppers, snap peas), severed
- 2 tbsps low-sodium soy sauce
- 1 tbsp sesame oil
- 2 pieces garlic, crushed
- 1 tsp ginger, grated
- Salt and pepper as required
- Sliced green onions for garnish (optional)

Directions:

1. Press tofu to take out excess moisture then cut it into cubes.
2. Inside your big griddle or wok, warm sesame oil inside a med-high temp.
3. Include cubed tofu then cook till golden brown on all sides. Take out from the griddle and put away.
4. Inside your similar griddle, include crushed garlic and grated ginger then sauté for around 30 secs.
5. Include mixed vegetables then cook for 5-7 mins 'til they are soft-crisp.
6. Stir in cauliflower rice then cook for an extra 3-4 mins, stirring constantly.
7. Return the cooked tofu to your griddle, include low-sodium soy sauce, and stir to blend.
8. Season using salt and pepper.
9. Garnish using sliced green onions if wanted prior to serving.

Per serving: Calories: 190kcal; Fat: 8g; Carbs: 13g; Protein: 16g

72. Turkey and Spinach Stuffed Bell Peppers

Preparation time: 20 mins

Cooking time: 40 mins

Servings: 4

Ingredients:

- 4 bell peppers, any color
- 1 lb. lean ground turkey
- 2 teacups fresh spinach, severed
- 1 teacup cooked brown rice
- 1 can (14 oz.) cubed tomatoes, drained
- 1/2 onion, severed
- 2 pieces garlic, crushed
- 1 tsp Italian seasoning
- Salt and pepper as required

Directions:

1. Warm up your oven to 375 deg.F.
2. Take out the seeds and membranes from the bell peppers and then slice off the tops of the peppers. Put away.
3. Inside your griddle, cook lean ground turkey inside a middling temp. till browned. Drain any excess fat.
4. Bring your severed onion and crushed garlic to your griddle then sauté for around 2-3 mins 'til they are softened.
5. Stir in fresh spinach then cook till wilted.
6. Take out the griddle from heat then include cooked brown rice, cubed tomatoes, Italian seasoning, salt, and pepper. Mix well.
7. Stuff each of your bell pepper with the turkey and spinach mixture.
8. Put your stuffed bell peppers in your baking dish and cover with aluminum foil.
9. Bake for 30-35 mins or 'til the bell peppers are soft.
10. Serve the turkey and spinach stuffed bell peppers hot.

Per serving: Calories: 300kcal; Fat: 6g; Carbs: 37g; Protein: 28g

73. Turkey and Sweet Potato Hash

Preparation time: 20 mins

Cooking time: 20 mins

Servings: 4

Ingredients:

- 1 lb. lean ground turkey
- 2 medium sweet potatoes, skinned and cubed
- 1 onion, severed
- 1 bell pepper, severed
- 2 pieces garlic, crushed
- 2 tbsps olive oil
- 1 tsp ground cumin
- 1/2 tsp paprika
- Salt and pepper as required
- Fresh parsley for garnish (optional)

Directions:

1. Inside your big griddle, warm olive oil inside a med-high temp.

2. Bring your severed onion and crushed garlic to your griddle then sauté for around 3-4 mins 'til they are softened.

3. Include cubed sweet potatoes then cook for around 10 mins, or 'til they are soft and mildly browned.

4. Push the sweet potatoes to one side of the griddle and include lean ground turkey to the other side. Cook the turkey till browned, breaking it apart with a spatula.

5. Stir in severed bell pepper, ground cumin, paprika, salt, and pepper.

6. Cook for an extra 5-7 mins till the bell pepper is soft.

7. Garnish using fresh parsley if wanted prior to serving.

Per serving: Calories: 280kcal; Fat: 10g; Carbs: 28g; Protein: 20g

74. Lentil and Vegetable Curry

Preparation time: 20 mins

Cooking time: 30 mins

Servings: 4

Ingredients:

- 1 teacup dried green or brown lentils, that is washed and drained
- 2 teacups vegetable broth (low-sodium)
- 1 can (14 oz.) cubed tomatoes (low-sodium)
- 2 teacups mixed vegetables (e.g., bell peppers, carrots, peas), severed
- 1 onion, severed
- 2 pieces garlic, crushed
- 2 tbsps olive oil
- 2 tbsps curry powder
- Salt and pepper as required
- Fresh cilantro for garnish (optional)

Directions:

1. Inside your saucepot, bring vegetable broth to a boil. Include lentils, decrease temp. to low, cover, then simmer for around 20-25 mins, or 'til lentils are soft and the liquid is engrossed.

2. While your lentils are cooking, warm olive oil in your big griddle inside a middling temp.

3. Bring your severed onion and crushed garlic to your griddle then sauté for around 3-4 mins 'til they are softened.

4. Stir in curry powder then cook for an extra 1-2 mins till fragrant.

5. Include mixed vegetables then cook for around 5-7 mins 'til they are soft.

6. Stir in your cubed tomatoes (with the juice) and the cooked lentils.

7. Season using salt and pepper then simmer for an extra 5 mins.

8. Garnish using fresh cilantro if wanted prior to serving.

Per serving: Calories: 300kcal; Fat: 7g; Carbs: 48g; Protein: 14g

75. Blackened Salmon with Roasted Brussels Sprouts

Preparation time: 15 mins

Cooking time: 20 mins

Servings: 4

Ingredients:

- 4 salmon fillets
- 1 lb. Brussels sprouts, clipped and divided
- 2 tbsps olive oil
- 1 tsp paprika
- 1/2 tsp cayenne pepper (adjust as required)
- 1/2 tsp garlic powder
- 1/2 tsp onion powder
- 1/2 tsp dried thyme
- Salt and pepper as required
- Lemon wedges for garnish (optional)

Directions:

1. Warm up your oven to 400 deg.F.

2. Inside your container, blend paprika, cayenne pepper, salt, garlic powder, onion powder, dried thyme, and pepper to create a blackening spice mix.

3. Toss Brussels sprouts using 1 tbsp of olive oil and half of the blackening spice mix.

4. Put your Brussels sprouts on your baking sheet and roast for around 15-20 mins, or 'til they are soft and mildly crispy.

5. While your Brussels sprouts are roasting, rub your salmon fillets using the remaining olive oil and the remaining blackening spice mix.

6. Heat your skillet in a medium-high heat then cook the salmon fillets for around 3-4 mins on all sides, or 'til they are cooked to your liking.

7. Serve the blackened salmon alongside the roasted Brussels sprouts.

8. Garnish using lemon wedges if wanted.

Per serving: Calories: 320kcal; Fat: 18g; Carbs: 14g; Protein: 26g

Snacks and Side Dishes Recipes

76. Grilled Veggie Skewers

Preparation time: 15 mins

Cooking time: 10 mins

Servings: 4

Ingredients:

- 2 zucchinis, sliced into rounds
- 1 red bell pepper, that is cut into chunks
- 1 yellow bell pepper, that is cut into chunks
- 1 red onion, that is cut into chunks
- 1 tbsp olive oil
- 1 tsp dried oregano
- Salt and pepper as required
- Wooden skewers, soaked in water

Directions:

1. Warm up your grill or stovetop griddle pan to med-high temp.

2. Thread the zucchini rounds, bell pepper chunks, and onion pieces onto the soaked wooden skewers, alternating between vegetables.

3. Inside your small container, mix the olive oil, dried oregano, salt, and pepper.

4. Brush the vegetable skewers using the olive oil mixture.

5. Grill the skewers for around 5 mins on all sides or 'til the vegetables are soft and have grill marks.

6. Serve warm.

Per serving: Calories: 80kcal; Fat: 3g; Carbs: 12g; Protein: 2g

77. Cucumber and Tomato Salad

Preparation time: 10 mins

Cooking time: 0 mins

Servings: 4

Ingredients:

- 2 cucumbers, cubed
- 2 tomatoes, cubed
- 1/4 red onion, finely severed
- 2 tbsps fresh lemon juice
- 1 tbsp olive oil
- Salt and pepper as required
- Fresh basil leaves for garnish (optional)

Directions:

1. Inside your big container, blend the cubed cucumbers, tomatoes, and red onion.

2. Inside your small container, whisk collectively the fresh lemon juice and olive oil.

3. Transfer the dressing over the cucumber and tomato mixture.

4. Season using salt and pepper as required.

5. Toss the salad to blend all of your ingredients.

6. Garnish using fresh basil leaves if wanted.

7. Serve chilled.

Per serving: Calories: 45kcal; Fat: 3g; Carbs: 5g; Protein: 1g

78. Baked Sweet Potato Fries

Preparation time: 15 mins

Cooking time: 25 mins

Servings: 4

Ingredients:

- 1 tbsp olive oil
- 1 tsp paprika
- 2 big sweet potatoes, that is cut into fine strips
- 1/2 tsp garlic powder
- Salt and pepper as required

Directions:

1. Warm up your oven to 425 deg. F then line your baking sheet using parchment paper.

2. Inside your big container, toss the sweet potato strips using olive oil, paprika, garlic powder, salt, and pepper till uniformly coated.

3. Disperse the sweet potato strips in a single layer on your prepared baking sheet.

4. Bake for around 25 mins, turning the fries halfway through, or 'til they are crispy and golden brown.

5. Serve warm.

Per serving: Calories: 100kcal; Fat: 3g; Carbs: 18g; Protein: 2g

79. Roasted Chickpeas

Preparation time: 5 mins

Cooking time: 30 mins

Servings: 4

Ingredients:

- 2 cans (15 oz. each) chickpeas, that is drained and washed
- 1 tbsp olive oil
- 1 tsp paprika
- 1/2 tsp cumin
- Salt and pepper as required

Directions:

1. Warm up your oven to 400 deg. F then line your baking sheet using parchment paper.

2. Inside your container, toss the chickpeas using olive oil, paprika, cumin, salt, and pepper till coated.

3. Disperse the chickpeas on your prepared baking sheet in a single layer.

4. Roast in the oven for around 30 mins, shaking the pan occasionally, 'til the chickpeas are crispy and golden brown.

5. Let them cool mildly prior to serving.

Per serving: Calories: 150kcal; Fat: 4g; Carbs: 21g; Protein: 7g

80. Grilled Asparagus Spears

Preparation time: 10 mins

Cooking time: 10 mins

Servings: 4

Ingredients:

- 1 bunch of asparagus spears, clipped
- 1 tbsp olive oil
- 1 piece garlic, crushed
- Zest of 1 lemon
- Salt and pepper as required

Directions:

1. Warm up your grill or stovetop griddle pan to med-high temp.

2. Inside your container, toss the asparagus using olive oil, salt, crushed garlic, lemon zest, and pepper.

3. Grill the asparagus for around 5 mins on all sides or 'til they are soft and have grill marks.

4. Serve warm.

Per serving: Calories: 30kcal; Fat: 2g; Carbs: 3g; Protein: 2g

81. Sautéed Spinach with Garlic

Preparation time: 5 mins

Cooking time: 5 mins

Servings: 4

Ingredients:

- 1 bunch of fresh spinach, that is washed and clipped
- 2 pieces garlic, crushed
- 1 tbsp olive oil
- Salt and pepper as required
- Lemon wedges for garnish (optional)

Directions:

1. Warm olive oil in your big griddle inside a med-high temp.

2. Include crushed garlic then sauté for around 30 secs or 'til fragrant.

3. Include the spinach to your griddle then cook, tossing frequently, till wilted (about 3-5 mins).

4. Season using salt and pepper as required.

5. Squeeze lemon juice over the spinach if wanted prior to serving.

Per serving: Calories: 30kcal; Fat: 2g; Carbs: 2g; Protein: 2g

82. Avocado and Tomato Salsa

Preparation time: 10 mins

Cooking time: 0 mins

Servings: 4

Ingredients:

- 2 ripe avocados, cubed
- 2 tomatoes, cubed
- 1/4 red onion, finely severed
- 2 tbsps fresh lime juice
- Fresh cilantro, severed
- Salt and pepper as required

Directions:

1. Inside your container, blend the cubed avocados, tomatoes, and red onion.

2. Spray with fresh lime juice and gently toss to coat.

3. Include your severed cilantro and season using salt and pepper as required.

4. Serve as a dip with whole-grain tortilla chips.

Per serving: Calories: 150kcal; Fat: 12g; Carbs: 10g; Protein: 2g

83. Baked Eggplant Chips

Preparation time: 15 mins

Cooking time: 20 mins

Servings: 4

Ingredients:

- 1 large eggplant, finely cut into rounds
- 2 tbsps olive oil
- 1/2 tsp smoked paprika
- 1/2 tsp dried thyme
- Salt and pepper as required

Directions:

1. Warm up your oven to 400 deg. F then line your baking sheet using parchment paper.

2. Inside your container, toss the eggplant slices using olive oil, smoked paprika, dried thyme, salt, and pepper till well-coated.

3. Organize the eggplant slices on your prepared baking sheet in a single layer.

4. Bake for 20 mins, flipping your slices halfway through, 'til they are crisp and golden.

5. Serve as a healthy alternative to potato chips.

Per serving: Calories: 60kcal; Fat: 5g; Carbs: 5g; Protein: 1g

84. Roasted Brussels Sprouts

Preparation time: 10 mins

Cooking time: 20 mins

Servings: 4

Ingredients:

- 1 lb. Brussels sprouts, clipped and divided
- 2 tbsps olive oil
- 1 tsp garlic powder
- Salt and pepper as required
- Grated Parmesan cheese (optional)

Directions:

1. Warm up your oven to 425 deg. F then line your baking sheet using parchment paper.

2. Inside your container, toss the Brussels sprouts using olive oil, garlic powder, salt, and pepper.

3. Disperse the Brussels sprouts on your prepared baking sheet in a single layer.

4. Roast for around 20 mins or 'til they are soft and lightly browned.

5. Optionally, spray using grated Parmesan cheese prior to serving.

Per serving: Calories: 70kcal; Fat: 5g; Carbs: 6g; Protein: 2g

85. Tuna and Cucumber Bites

Preparation time: 10 mins

Cooking time: 0 mins

Servings: 4

Ingredients:

- 1 can (5 oz.) tuna, drained
- 1 cucumber, sliced into rounds
- 2 tbsps Greek yogurt
- 1 tbsp Dijon mustard
- Fresh dill, for garnish (optional)
- Salt and pepper as required

Directions:

1. Inside your container, mix the drained tuna, Greek yogurt, Dijon mustard, salt, and pepper till well blended.

2. Put your spoonful of the tuna mixture on each cucumber round.

3. Garnish using fresh dill if wanted.

4. Serve as a light and protein-rich appetizer.

Per serving: Calories: 70kcal; Fat: 2g; Carbs: 2g; Protein: 12g

86. Steamed Broccoli with Lemon

Preparation time: 10 mins

Cooking time: 5 mins

Servings: 4

Ingredients:

- 1 lb. broccoli florets
- Zest and juice of 1 lemon
- 1 tbsp olive oil
- 2 pieces garlic, crushed
- Salt and pepper as required

Directions:

1. Steam the broccoli florets till soft, about 5 mins.

2. Inside your container, mix the lemon zest, lemon juice, salt, olive oil, crushed garlic, and pepper.

3. Spray the lemon mixture over the steamed broccoli.

4. Toss to coat the broccoli uniformly.

5. Serve as a nutritious side dish.

Per serving: Calories: 45kcal; Fat: 3g; Carbs: 4g; Protein: 2g

87. Cabbage and Carrot Slaw

Preparation time: 10 mins

Cooking time: 0 mins

Servings: 4

Ingredients:

- 4 teacups shredded green cabbage
- 1 teacup shredded carrots
- 2 tbsps Greek yogurt
- 1 tbsp apple cider vinegar
- 1 tsp honey
- Salt and pepper as required

Directions:

1. Inside your big container, blend the shredded cabbage and carrots.

2. Inside your small container, whisk collectively the Greek yogurt, apple cider vinegar, honey, salt, and pepper.

3. Transfer the dressing over the cabbage and carrots.

4. Toss to coat the slaw uniformly.

5. Serve chilled as a crunchy and refreshing side.

Per serving: Calories: 45kcal; Fat: 0g; Carbs: 11g; Protein: 1g

88. Greek Cucumber Cups

Preparation time: 10 mins

Cooking time: 0 mins

Servings: 4

Ingredients:

- 2 cucumbers
- 1 teacup cherry tomatoes, divided
- 1/2 teacup crumbled feta cheese
- 1/4 teacup Kalamata olives, that is pitted and severed
- 2 tbsps fresh lemon juice
- Fresh mint leaves for garnish (optional)
- Salt and pepper as required

Directions:

1. Slice the cucumbers into 1" thick rounds.

2. Use a small spoon to scoop out a portion of the center of each cucumber round to create a teacup.

3. Inside your container, blend the cherry tomatoes, feta cheese, and severed Kalamata olives.

4. Spray fresh lemon juice over the mixture and toss to blend.

5. Season using salt and pepper as required.

6. Fill each cucumber teacup with the tomato and feta mixture.

7. Garnish using fresh mint leaves if wanted.

8. Serve as a refreshing and low-calorie appetizer.

Per serving: Calories: 90kcal; Fat: 6g; Carbs: 7g; Protein: 4g

89. Sautéed Mushrooms with Garlic

Preparation time: 10 mins

Cooking time: 10 mins

Servings: 4

Ingredients:

- 1 pound mushrooms, sliced
- 2 tbsps olive oil
- 2 pieces garlic, crushed
- Fresh parsley, severed, for garnish (optional)
- Salt and pepper as required

Directions:

1. Warm olive oil in your skillet inside a med-high temp.

2. Include the sliced mushrooms then sauté 'til they release their moisture and turn golden brown (about 8-10 mins).

3. Include crushed garlic to your griddle then sauté for an extra 1-2 mins, till fragrant.

4. Season using salt and pepper as required.

5. Garnish using fresh severed parsley if wanted.

6. Serve as a flavorful and low-calorie side dish.

Per serving: Calories: 60kcal; Fat: 5g; Carbs: 4g; Protein: 3g

90. Cilantro Lime Coleslaw

Preparation time: 10 mins

Cooking time: 0 mins

Servings: 4

Ingredients:

- 4 teacups shredded green cabbage
- 1/2 teacup severed fresh cilantro
- 2 tbsps Greek yogurt
- Juice of 2 limes
- 1 tbsp honey
- Salt and pepper as required

Directions:

1. Inside your big container, blend the shredded cabbage and severed cilantro.

2. Inside your small container, whisk collectively the Greek yogurt, lime juice, honey, salt, and pepper.

3. Transfer the dressing over the cabbage and cilantro.

4. Toss to coat the coleslaw uniformly.

5. Serve chilled as a tangy and refreshing side dish.

Per serving: Calories: 40kcal; Fat: 0g; Carbs: 10g; Protein: 1g

91. Roasted Red Pepper Hummus

Preparation time: 10 mins

Cooking time: 25 mins (roasting peppers)

Servings: 4

Ingredients:

- 2 red bell peppers
- 1 can (15 oz.) chickpeas, that is drained and washed
- 2 pieces garlic
- 2 tbsps tahini
- Juice of 1 lemon
- 2 tbsps olive oil
- 1/2 tsp cumin
- Salt and pepper as required

Directions:

1. Warm up your oven to 450 deg.F.

2. Put your red bell peppers on your baking sheet then roast for around 25 mins, mixing irregularly, 'til they are charred and soft.

3. Take out the peppers from your oven, let them cool, then peel, seed, and chop them.

4. In your food processor, blend the roasted red peppers, chickpeas, garlic, tahini, lemon juice, olive oil, cumin, salt, and pepper.

5. Blend till smooth and creamy.

6. Serve as a flavorful dip with vegetable sticks or whole-grain crackers.

Per serving: Calories: 150kcal; Fat: 9g; Carbs: 15g; Protein: 4g

92. Baked Cauliflower Bites

Preparation time: 15 mins

Cooking time: 25 mins

Servings: 4

Ingredients:

- 1 head cauliflower, cut into florets
- 2 tbsps olive oil
- 1 tsp smoked paprika
- 1/2 tsp garlic powder
- Salt and pepper as required

Directions:

1. Warm up your oven to 425 deg. F then line your baking sheet using parchment paper.

2. Inside your container, toss the cauliflower florets using olive oil, smoked paprika, garlic powder, salt, and pepper 'til they are thoroughly covered.

3. Disperse the cauliflower on your prepared baking sheet in a single layer.

4. Bake for around 25 mins or 'til they are soft and mildly crispy.

5. Serve as a healthy alternative to traditional fried snacks.

Per serving: Calories: 60kcal; Fat: 5g; Carbs: 5g; Protein: 2g

93. Spinach and Feta Stuffed Mushrooms

Preparation time: 15 mins

Cooking time: 20 mins

Servings: 4

Ingredients:

- 16 large button mushrooms, stems removed
- 2 teacups fresh spinach, severed
- 1/2 teacup crumbled feta cheese
- 2 pieces garlic, crushed
- 1 tbsp olive oil
- Salt and pepper as required

Directions:

1. Warm up your oven to 375 deg. F then line your baking sheet using parchment paper.

2. Inside your griddle, warm olive oil inside a middling temp. Include crushed garlic and severed spinach, then sauté till the spinach is wilted.

3. Take out your skillet from heat then stir in the crumbled feta cheese.

4. Stuff each of your mushroom cap with the spinach and feta mixture.

5. Put your stuffed mushrooms on the baking sheet.

6. Bake for around 20 mins or 'til the mushrooms are soft then the filling is heated through.

7. Serve as a savory and protein-rich appetizer.

Per serving: Calories: 70kcal; Fat: 5g; Carbs: 4g; Protein: 3g

94. Roasted Beet and Walnut Salad

Preparation time: 15 mins

Cooking time: 45 mins (roasting beets)

Servings: 4

Ingredients:

- 4 medium-sized beets, skinned and cubed
- 1/2 teacup walnuts, severed
- 4 teacups mixed greens (e.g., spinach, arugula)
- 2 tbsps balsamic vinegar
- 2 tbsps olive oil
- Salt and pepper as required
- Crumbled goat cheese (optional)

Directions:

1. Warm up your oven to 400 deg.F.

2. Toss the cubed beets using olive oil, salt, and pepper.

3. Disperse the beets on your baking sheet and roast for around 45 mins or 'til they are soft and caramelized.

4. Inside your container, blend the roasted beets, severed walnuts, mixed greens, balsamic vinegar, and olive oil.

5. Toss to coat all ingredients.

6. Optionally, top with crumbled goat cheese prior to serving.

7. Serve as a colorful and nutritious salad.

Per serving: Calories: 180kcal; Fat: 14g; Carbs: 11g; Protein: 3g

95. Cucumber and Avocado Salsa

Preparation time: 10 mins

Cooking time: 0 mins

Servings: 4

Ingredients:

- 2 cucumbers, cubed
- 2 ripe avocados, cubed
- 1/4 red onion, finely severed
- 2 tbsps fresh lime juice
- 2 tbsps fresh cilantro, severed
- Salt and pepper as required

Directions:

1. Inside your container, blend the cubed cucumbers, cubed avocados, and finely severed red onion.

2. Spray fresh lime juice over the mixture.

3. Include your severed cilantro and season using salt and pepper as required.

4. Toss to blend all ingredients.

5. Serve chilled as a cool and creamy salsa.

Per serving: Calories: 150kcal; Fat: 13g; Carbs: 10g; Protein: 2g

96. Steamed Artichoke with Lemon Herb Dipping Sauce

Preparation time: 10 mins

Cooking time: 30 mins (steaming)

Servings: 4

Ingredients:

- 4 big artichokes
- 2 tbsps fresh lemon juice
- 1/4 teacup Greek yogurt
- 1 tbsp fresh parsley, severed
- 1 tsp fresh dill, severed
- 1 clove garlic, crushed
- Salt and pepper as required

Directions:

1. Trim the stems of your artichokes then take out any tough outer leaves.

2. Steam the artichokes for around 30 mins or 'til the leaves can be simply pulled off.

3. Inside your container, blend the fresh lemon juice, Greek yogurt, severed parsley, severed dill, crushed garlic, salt, and pepper to make the dipping sauce.

4. Serve the steamed artichokes with the lemon herb dipping sauce for a unique and healthy snack or side.

Per serving: Calories: 60kcal; Fat: 1g; Carbs: 13g; Protein: 3g

97. Roasted Radishes

Preparation time: 10 mins

Cooking time: 20 mins

Servings: 4

Ingredients:

- 2 bunches of radishes, clipped and divided
- 2 tbsps olive oil
- 1 tsp dried thyme
- Salt and pepper as required

Directions:

1. Warm up your oven to 425 deg. F then line your baking sheet using parchment paper.

2. Toss the divided radishes using olive oil, dried thyme, salt, and pepper inside a container.

3. Disperse the radishes on your prepared baking sheet in a single layer.

4. Roast for around 20 mins or 'til they are soft and mildly crispy.

5. Serve as a unique and low-calorie side dish.

Per serving: Calories: 40kcal; Fat: 3g; Carbs: 3g; Protein: 1g

98. Cucumber and Radish Salad

Preparation time: 10 mins

Cooking time: 0 mins

Servings: 4

Ingredients:

- 2 cucumbers, finely cut
- 1 bunch of radishes, finely cut
- 1/4 red onion, finely cut
- 2 tbsps fresh dill, severed
- 2 tbsps white wine vinegar
- 1 tbsp olive oil
- Salt and pepper as required

Directions:

1. In your huge bowl, blend the cucumber slices, radish slices, finely cut red onion, and severed fresh dill.

2. Inside your small container, whisk collectively the white wine vinegar, olive oil, salt, and pepper.

3. Transfer the dressing over the salad and toss to coat all ingredients.

4. Serve chilled as a refreshing and low-calorie side dish.

Per serving: Calories: 45kcal; Fat: 3g; Carbs: 4g; Protein: 1g

99. Steamed Green Beans with Almonds

Preparation time: 10 mins

Cooking time: 10 mins (steaming)

Servings: 4

Ingredients:

- 1 lb. green beans, clipped
- 2 tbsps slivered almonds
- 1 tbsp olive oil
- 1 tsp lemon zest
- Salt and pepper as required

Directions:

1. Steam your green beans for 10 mins or 'til they are crisp-soft.

2. Inside your griddle, toast the slivered almonds inside a middling temp. 'til they are lightly browned (around 2-3 mins). Take out from heat.

3. Inside your container, toss the steamed green beans using olive oil, lemon zest, toasted almonds, salt, and pepper.

4. Serve as a simple and nutritious side dish.

Per serving: Calories: 70kcal; Fat: 5g; Carbs: 6g; Protein: 2g

100. Spicy Roasted Chickpeas

Preparation time: 10 mins

Cooking time: 30 mins

Servings: 4

Ingredients:

• 2 cans (15 oz. each) chickpeas, that is drained and washed

• 2 tbsps olive oil

• 1 tsp smoked paprika

• 1/2 tsp cayenne pepper (adjust as required)

• Salt and pepper as required

Directions:

1. Warm up your oven to 400 deg. F then line your baking sheet using parchment paper.

2. Inside your container, toss the chickpeas using olive oil, smoked paprika, cayenne pepper, salt, and pepper 'til they are thoroughly covered.

3. Disperse the chickpeas on your prepared baking sheet in a single layer.

4. Roast for around 30 mins or 'til they are crispy and golden brown.

5. Serve as a spicy and protein-rich snack.

Per serving: Calories: 160kcal; Fat: 5g; Carbs: 23g; Protein: 6g

Long-Term Success and Persistence

Cardiovascular Exercise

Cardiovascular exercises, often referred to as "cardio," are a cornerstone of promoting health and well-being, especially for individuals with an endomorphic body type. Endomorphs naturally have a predisposition to store fat, making it essential for them to include regular cardio exercises as a crucial component of their fitness regimen. These exercises provide a wide array of benefits, including improvements in cardiovascular health, increased calorie burning, and an overall boost in fitness levels.

High-Intensity Interval Training (HIIT)

High-Intensity Interval Training, or HIIT, is a fitness technique characterized by alternating short bursts of vigorous activity with brief periods of rest or lower-intensity exercise. This approach is particularly advantageous for individuals with an endomorphic body type because it helps elevate their metabolism and burn calories efficiently. Additionally, HIIT contributes to the development of lean muscle mass, which, in turn, can enhance the body's metabolic rate.

Benefits of HIIT

- **Effective Calorie Burning:** HIIT workouts excel in burning calories, making them instrumental in weight management for endomorphs.

- **Metabolism Booster:** This form of training elevates metabolism, leading to continued calorie burn even when at rest.

- **Cardiovascular Endurance:** HIIT enhances cardiovascular fitness, improving the heart's ability to pump blood and oxygen efficiently.

- **Time Efficiency:** HIIT sessions are relatively short but highly effective, making them a suitable choice for those with busy schedules.

Running on The Treadmill

Treadmill running is a timeless and versatile cardio exercise that allows individuals to tailor the intensity to their fitness level. Endomorphs can greatly benefit from treadmill running as it engages major muscle groups and facilitates calorie expenditure.

Benefits of Treadmill Running

- **Calorie Burn:** Treadmill running burns calories effectively, contributing to weight loss efforts.

- **Cardiovascular Improvement:** It enhances cardiovascular fitness, improving the heart and lung functions.

- **Adaptability:** Treadmill speed and incline can be adjusted to accommodate various fitness levels and goals.

- **Joint-Friendly:** Running on a treadmill has a lower impact on joints compared to running on hard outdoor surfaces.

Cycling/Spinning

Cycling, whether performed outdoors or in a spinning class, offers a low-impact yet highly effective cardio workout for endomorphs. This activity engages multiple muscle groups, including the legs, core, and upper body.

Benefits of Cycling/Spinning

• **Enhanced Cardiovascular Endurance:** It improves the heart's ability to pump blood and oxygen efficiently throughout the body.

• **Effective Calorie Burn:** Cycling effectively burns calories, aiding in weight management.

• **Joint-Friendly:** It is a low-impact exercise, reducing the strain on joints compared to high-impact activities.

• **Leg Strength and Toning:** Regular cycling enhances leg strength and contributes to well-defined leg muscles.

Boating

Boating can provide a unique and enjoyable form of cardiovascular exercise, especially when engaging in activities like kayaking or rowing. These activities primarily target the upper body and core muscles while allowing individuals to connect with nature and scenic surroundings.

Benefits of Boating

• **Upper Body and Core Engagement:** Paddling engages the muscles of the upper body and core, promoting strength and endurance.

• **Serene Workout Environment:** Boating offers a serene and enjoyable workout environment, reducing stress and enhancing mental well-being.

• **Arm and Shoulder Strength:** Consistent boating can lead to increased arm and shoulder strength, improving overall upper body fitness.

Swimming

Swimming stands out as a highly efficient full-body workout that provides low-impact cardiovascular advantages, making it an excellent choice for individuals with an endomorphic body type. It combines aerobic exercise with resistance training in the water.

Benefits of Swimming

• **Full-Body Toning:** Swimming tones muscles throughout the body, promoting a lean and sculpted physique.

• **Improved Cardiovascular Fitness:** Regular swimming sessions enhance cardiovascular fitness, improving the efficiency of the heart and lungs.

• **Joint-Friendly:** Swimming is gentle on the joints, reducing the risk of impact-related injuries.

• **Weight Management:** It aids in weight management by burning calories and increasing metabolic activity.

Cardio Dance

Cardio dance classes, such as Zumba or aerobics, blend dance movements with cardiovascular exercises, offering a fun and engaging way for endomorphs to improve their cardiovascular fitness while enjoying music and dance.

Benefits of Cardio Dance

• **Coordination and Balance:** Cardio dance enhances coordination and balance through dynamic movements and rhythmic patterns.

• **Calorie Burn:** It burns calories effectively, supporting weight management goals.

• **Mood Enhancement:** Dancing to music can boost mood, reduce stress, and increase overall well-being.

• **Social Experience:** Cardio dance classes provide a social and enjoyable exercise environment, fostering a sense of community and motivation.

Incorporating these diverse cardiovascular exercises into a fitness routine can be highly beneficial for individuals with an endomorphic body type. It's essential to select activities that are enjoyable and sustainable to ensure long-term adherence to a fitness regimen. Additionally, pairing cardio workouts with a balanced diet is key to achieving and maintaining a healthy weight and overall well-being for endomorphs.

Strength Training

Strength training stands as an essential pillar within the realm of fitness, especially for individuals possessing an endomorphic body type. Endomorphs, characterized by a higher proportion of body fat, often encounter formidable challenges when it comes to shedding weight and maintaining a lean and toned physique. However, with the strategic inclusion of specific strength training exercises, this journey can become far more attainable, and the desired fitness objectives can be well within reach.

Squats

Squats serve as the very bedrock upon which strength training is built. This compound exercise exerts its influence over an array of muscle groups, with a particular emphasis on the quadriceps, hamstrings, glutes, and lower back. For endomorphs, squats are a goldmine of advantages:

• **Building leg and glute strength:** Squats emerge as a formidable weapon for fortifying the lower body, bestowing upon it a newfound vitality, enhancing overall functional fitness, and bestowing unwavering stability.

• **Elevating metabolism:** Rooted in their compound nature, squats emerge as prolific calorie-burners, an invaluable asset in the world of weight management, as they actively contribute to the melting away of excess pounds.

• **Enhancing core stability:** The proper execution of squats mandates the active engagement of core muscles, thereby fostering the development of a strong, resilient midsection, bolstering the body's core stability.

Deadlifts from The Ground

Deadlifts occupy a similar echelon in the realm of compound exercises. They engage a multitude of muscle groups, including the lower back, glutes, hamstrings, and core. For endomorphs, deadlifts bring with them a trove of advantages:

• **Fortifying overall strength:** Deadlifts offer a holistic, full-body workout, leading to remarkable gains in terms of strength and muscle mass, thereby sculpting a more formidable physique.

• **Facilitating fat loss:** The sheer intensity of deadlifts translates into a substantial calorie expenditure, acting as a powerful ally in the pursuit of weight management.

• **Uplifting posture and back health:** Executed with proper form, deadlifts become an invaluable tool for fortifying the muscles of the back, simultaneously reducing the risk of injury and contributing to the betterment of posture.

Flat Bench

The flat bench press, an iconic upper-body exercise, squarely targets the chest, shoulders, and triceps. For endomorphs, the benefits of incorporating flat bench presses are multifaceted:

• **Cultivating upper body strength:** Bench presses become instrumental in endowing endomorphs with a robust chest and upper body, providing a solid foundation for further fitness endeavors.

• **Elevating metabolism:** Engaging a plethora of muscle groups during flat bench presses significantly contributes to calorie incineration, a key factor in weight control.

• **Enhancing chest aesthetics:** The consistent inclusion of bench presses in one's workout regimen can work wonders in refining the appearance of the chest, serving as a cornerstone in the quest for a harmonious physique.

Exercises with Elastic Bands

The incorporation of elastic bands into one's fitness routine brings forth a world of versatility, making them an ideal choice for endomorphs seeking comprehensive improvements. The advantages of these elastic band workouts are manifold:

• **Low-impact option:** Elastic band exercises exhibit a gentle disposition towards joints, making them an ideal choice for individuals with varying fitness levels and those who prioritize the preservation of joint health.

• **Bolstering muscular endurance:** The repetitive movements involving resistance bands lead to an augmentation of muscular endurance, enabling endomorphs to carry out daily activities with heightened efficiency.

• **Fostering flexibility:** The introduction of resistance bands into one's exercise repertoire bestows an increase in flexibility, thereby mitigating the risk of injury and facilitating enhanced mobility on the whole.

Pull-Ups/Push-Ups

Pull-ups and push-ups, quintessential bodyweight exercises, are honed to target the upper body, encompassing the back, chest, shoulders, and arms. For endomorphs, these exercises present a plethora of advantages:

• **Strengthening upper body muscles:** Both pull-ups and push-ups serve as potent tools for fortifying upper body strength, sculpting well-defined muscles, and heightening physical prowess.

• **Championing functional fitness:** These exercises faithfully emulate the movements encountered in the course of everyday life, catalyzing an all-encompassing improvement in overall physical capabilities.

• **Contributing to weight management:** The consistent practice of pull-ups and push-ups unfailingly results in a substantial calorie expenditure, making meaningful strides towards the realm of fat loss. Strength training exercises play a crucial role in helping endomorphs achieve their fitness goals. Squats, deadlifts from the ground, flat bench presses, exercises with elastic bands, and bodyweight exercises like pull-ups and push-ups provide numerous benefits, including improved strength, enhanced metabolism, better aesthetics, injury prevention, and functional fitness. Incorporating these exercises into a well-rounded fitness routine can help endomorphs build a healthier and more balanced physique.

Other Activities

Integrating a diverse range of exercises into your fitness regimen is crucial, particularly if you're an endomorph seeking to control your body composition and enhance your overall health.

Fast Walk

Fast walking, also referred to as brisk walking, entails moving at a pace considerably quicker than a leisurely stroll. It's an exercise characterized by its low-impact nature, rendering it accessible to nearly everyone, regardless of fitness level or location.

Benefits

• **Fat Burning:** Engaging in fast walking induces an elevation in heart rate, leading to an increased calorie expenditure. This, in turn, promotes fat loss, with a particular emphasis on reducing abdominal fat.

• **Improved Cardiovascular Health:** Consistent participation in brisk walking serves as an effective means of strengthening the heart, lowering blood pressure, and enhancing overall cardiovascular fitness.

• **Low Impact:** Unlike high-impact activities such as running, fast walking is gentle on your joints, mitigating the risk of injury.

• **Stress Reduction:** Embarking on outdoor fast walks, especially in natural settings, can foster mental relaxation and substantially alleviate stress levels.

Go Upstairs

Stair climbing is an exemplary exercise that heavily engages the muscles in your glutes, legs, and core. The versatility of this activity allows you to partake in it at home, within a gym setting, or even within tall buildings equipped with staircases.

Benefits

• **Lower Body Strength:** Ascending stairs calls upon the quadriceps, hamstrings, calves, and glutes to work harmoniously, ultimately contributing to the toning and fortification of these crucial muscle groups.

- **Calorie Burn:** Stair climbing proves to be a highly efficient method for burning calories and enhancing your metabolic rate.
- **Cardiovascular Workout:** The act of climbing stairs causes your heart rate to rise, conferring cardiovascular benefits akin to those achieved through running or cycling.
- **Functional Fitness:** This exercise markedly improves your capacity to perform day-to-day activities that involve negotiating stairs or inclines, thereby enhancing your functional fitness.

Jumping Rope

Jumping rope entails the use of a skipping rope, with participants jumping over it as it rotates beneath their feet. This seemingly simple exercise is, in fact, highly effective.

Benefits

- **Calorie Torching:** Jumping rope is renowned for its calorie-burning prowess, making it a valuable asset in weight management efforts.
- **Cardiovascular Fitness:** It provides an intense cardiovascular workout, which in turn bolsters the strength and endurance of your heart and lungs.
- **Coordination:** Regular sessions of jumping rope significantly enhance coordination, agility, and balance.
- **Full-Body Engagement:** The exercise targets various muscle groups, including the legs, core, and upper body, ensuring a comprehensive workout experience.

Boxing

Boxing, both as a combat sport and a fitness activity, involves actions like punching bags, mitt work, or sparring with a partner. It seamlessly blends aerobic and anaerobic elements, making it a versatile exercise option.

Benefits

- **Total-Body Workout:** Boxing engages a wide spectrum of muscle groups, encompassing the upper body (shoulders, arms, chest), core, and lower body (legs and hips). This holistic engagement promotes overall strength and muscle tone.
- **Fat Loss:** The high-intensity nature of boxing accelerates the process of shedding excess fat, with a pronounced effect on reducing fat around the midsection.
- **Stress Relief:** The physical exertion and mental focus demanded by boxing serve as a potent stress reliever, helping to alleviate tension and anxiety.
- **Improved Coordination:** Regular practice of boxing heightens hand-eye coordination and enhances reflexes.
- **Cardiovascular Conditioning:** Boxing sessions elevate your heart rate, making a significant contribution to cardiovascular fitness enhancement.

Incorporating these diverse exercises into your fitness routine is instrumental in assisting endomorphs in achieving their health and fitness aspirations. However, it is imperative to bear in mind that consistency and a well-balanced diet are pivotal factors in achieving and sustaining a healthy body composition

Role of Stress and Sleep

Stress, often associated with negative connotations, is, in fact, a fundamental response that has evolved in both humans and animals over millennia. It serves a crucial purpose in preparing the organism to cope with important or dangerous situations.

In humans, stress triggers a complex chain of physiological events orchestrated by the autonomic nervous system (ANS). The ANS releases hormones, such as adrenaline and cortisol, into the bloodstream. These hormones play a pivotal role in preparing the body to respond swiftly and effectively to perceived threats. One of the immediate effects is the elevation of heart rate, ensuring a more efficient circulation of blood to vital organs and muscles. This heightened state of physiological readiness is often referred to as the "fight-or-flight" response, an evolutionary adaptation that was essential for human survival during earlier stages of development.

In contemporary society, however, stressors have evolved beyond life-threatening situations. Modern challenges, such as problems at work or difficulties in relationships, can still trigger the same fight-or-flight response, even though they may not pose an immediate threat to one's survival.

The impact of stress becomes particularly concerning when it persists over an extended period. While it is normal to experience occasional stress, chronic stress can lead to the nervous system remaining in a constant state of heightened arousal. This prolonged activation of the stress response can have severe and far-reaching consequences for both physical and mental health.

One of the significant effects of chronic stress is sleep deprivation. Constantly being on high alert can make it difficult to initiate and maintain restful sleep. Racing and anxious thoughts at night further exacerbate the problem. This lack of restorative sleep, in turn, can contribute to a vicious cycle of stress, as insufficient sleep can increase stress levels and make it even harder to cope.

Research underscores the prevalence of stress-related sleep disturbances. According to a National Sleep Foundation survey, a significant 43 percent of individuals aged 13–64 have reported experiencing difficulty falling asleep or staying asleep due to stress almost once in the past month.

Stress, originally an adaptive mechanism for survival, continues to play a role in modern life. While it once helped our ancestors confront physical threats, today's stressors often revolve around complex emotional and social challenges. When stress becomes chronic, it can disrupt sleep patterns and contribute to a cascade of physical and psychological health issues. Recognizing and managing stress is essential for maintaining overall well-being in our contemporary, fast-paced world.

Yoga

Yoga, rooted in ancient traditions, represents a holistic approach to exercise, prioritizing the synchronization of conscious breathing, flexibility enhancement, and strength development. Beyond its physical aspects, yoga extends its influence to the realms of spirituality, mental well-being, and physical health, making it a multifaceted discipline that caters to various individual preferences and needs.

Within the vast landscape of yoga, diverse styles exist, catering to individuals with varying inclinations. Some forms of yoga emphasize the spiritual aspect, incorporating meditation and mindfulness practices, while others adhere to a more secular approach, focusing primarily on physical postures and breathing techniques. This flexibility in style ensures that yoga remains accessible and adaptable to the diverse range of practitioners.

Yoga's multifaceted nature also extends to its physical demands. Some yoga styles are gentle and emphasize relaxation and stretching, promoting a sense of calm and mental clarity. In contrast, other forms of yoga are physically demanding, challenging practitioners to enhance their endurance, stamina, and muscle strength. Thus, yoga accommodates both those seeking tranquility and those pursuing a more rigorous physical workout.

In terms of its potential benefits, a comprehensive review conducted in 2020 analyzed prior research and yielded promising results regarding the impact of yoga on sleep quality, particularly among women grappling with insomnia. Researchers observed that yoga, with its blend of physical postures, relaxation techniques, and breath control, proved especially advantageous for individuals experiencing menopausal symptoms, highlighting its relevance across various life stages.

While not every study included in the analysis demonstrated a definitive positive effect of yoga on sleep, the reassuring finding was that yoga did not produce any adverse effects. This suggests that integrating yoga into one's routine may constitute a relatively low-risk strategy for improving sleep, serving as an initial option prior to considering more invasive or pharmacological treatments.

In addition to its sleep-related benefits, a research review from 2019 explored the realm of mind-body therapies, including yoga, in alleviating insomnia severity. The findings were consistent with the notion that yoga, as a mind-body practice, can significantly reduce the severity of insomnia symptoms based on previous studies, further underscoring its potential as a therapeutic tool for addressing sleep issues.

Yoga's ancient roots and versatile nature position it as a valuable tool for enhancing spiritual, mental, and physical health. Its adaptability in terms of style and physical intensity makes it accessible to a wide range of individuals. Moreover, emerging research suggests that yoga can play a beneficial role in promoting better sleep and managing insomnia, offering a natural and low-risk option for those seeking improved sleep quality and overall well-being.

Which type of yoga helps with insomnia?

Yoga can be a valuable tool in promoting better sleep, but not all types of yoga are equally effective in this regard. While some forms of yoga, such as hot yoga and Vinyasa, are known for their high-intensity nature and potential to increase heart rate and energy levels, which might not be conducive to sleep, there are specific types of yoga that can indeed help improve sleep quality and address sleep-related issues.

Here are some low-intensity forms of yoga that are particularly helpful for improving sleep:

1. **Gentle Hatha Yoga:** Hatha yoga encompasses various subtypes, but the common thread is the practice of moving the body slowly through different postures while synchronizing each movement with the breath. Gentle Hatha yoga, in particular, emphasizes slower and less active movements, making it an excellent choice for a pre-sleep practice. The gentle, deliberate stretches and controlled breathing can help relax the body and mind, preparing you for a restful night's sleep.

2. **Restorative or Yin Yoga:** Restorative yoga and Yin yoga are both designed to promote deep stretching and relaxation. In these practices, participants hold passive poses for an extended period, often with the support of props like blankets or bolsters. This slow and meditative approach helps release tension in the muscles and calm the nervous system, making it an ideal choice for winding down prior to bedtime.

3. **Yoga Nidra:** Yoga Nidra is a unique form of yoga that aims to induce a state of deep relaxation and conscious sleep. During a Yoga Nidra session, you lie down in a comfortable position then follow a guided meditation that takes you into a state between wakefulness and slumber. This practice is known for its ability to reduce stress, anxiety, and insomnia. In fact, a 2020 study found that a daily 11-minute Yoga Nidra practice resulted in improved stress levels and sleep quality after just 30 days.

Some yoga postures that can assist an individual in unwinding prior to bedtime comprise:

Legs Up The Wall (Viparita Karani)

To execute this pose:

1. Start by sitting sideways against a wall, with your legs extended straight in front of you.

2. Exhale as you lower your upper body to the floor and swing your legs up and over your body, allowing them to rest against the wall.

3. Keep your arms alongside your body with your palms facing upward.

4. Optionally, you can place a cushion under your sacrum for lower back support.

5. To stretch your inner thighs, you can also let your legs fall open while they are against the wall in this pose.

Child's Pose (Balasana)

To perform this pose:

1. Kneel on the floor, ensuring that the tops of your feet are flat against the ground.

2. Keep your knees and feet together, with your big toes touching.

3. Sit on your heels.

4. Lean forward, folding your spine over your legs so that your forehead touches the floor or comes close to it. You can use a block beneath your forehead if needed.

5. Your arms can either rest at your sides or extend in front of your body with your palms facing down.

6. If desired, widen your knees and allow your upper body to rest between your thighs, keeping the big toes touching.

7. Relax in this position for as long as it feels comfortable, and focus on your breath.

Reclined Butterfly Pose (Supta Baddha Konasana)

To execute this pose:

1. Lie down on your back, extending your legs and arms straight.

2. Bend your knees and bring your feet towards your pelvis, so that the soles of your feet touch each other.

3. Interlock your fingers and place them on your stomach.

4. Stay in this position while maintaining mindfulness of your breath.

Corpse Pose (Savasana): Conclude your routine with Corpse Pose, which can be an excellent posture for meditation at the conclusion of a yoga session.

To practice this pose:

1. Lie flat on your back.

2. Straighten your legs and arms.

3. Keep your hands open with palms facing upward.

4. Allow your ankles to naturally fall apart.

5. Take a deep breath then relax your muscles.

6. Continue to focus on your breath. When you're ready to conclude, gently flex your hands and feet to reawaken your body. Then, roll onto one side and sit up gradually.

These yoga poses can help you relax and prepare your body and mind for a restful night's sleep.

Tips for starting with yoga

Starting a yoga practice, even with short sessions, can be a valuable way to reduce stress and improve your sleep quality. Here are some tips to help you begin your yoga journey:

1. **Choose a Regular Time:** Establishing a consistent practice is key to reaping the benefits of yoga. Select a specific time for your yoga practice, ideally not too close to bedtime, and strive to adhere to this schedule every day. For instance, you might decide to do yoga half an hour prior to your bedtime routine begins.

2. **Create a Calm Environment:** Setting the right atmosphere can greatly enhance your yoga experience. Consider dimming the lights, playing soothing ambient music, or using essential oils to diffuse calming scents while you practice. This can create a tranquil ambiance and help establish a positive connection between yoga and sleep in your mind.

3. **Wear Comfortable Nightwear:** Instead of changing in and out of yoga attire, opt for loose-fitting nightwear that allows you to transition seamlessly from your yoga practice to sleep. This eliminates the need for additional steps and helps maintain the relaxation achieved during your yoga session.

4. **Start Slowly:** If you're new to yoga or have difficulty concentrating for extended periods, it's perfectly fine to begin with short sessions. Starting slowly allows you to build a strong foundation and gradually progress. You can initiate your practice with brief routines and later expand your practice as you become more comfortable and confident.

5. **Focus on Consistency:** Consistency is key in yoga. Even if your sessions are short initially, aim to practice regularly. Consistent practice can lead to improvements in flexibility, strength, and mental well-being over time.

6. **Listen to Your Body:** Pay close attention to your body and its signals. Yoga should be a gentle and mindful practice. If you experience discomfort or pain, modify poses or seek guidance from a qualified yoga instructor to ensure you're practicing safely.

7. **Explore Different Styles:** Yoga offers a wide range of styles and practices. Don't hesitate to explore various forms of yoga, such as Hatha, Vinyasa, Restorative, or Yin yoga, to discover what resonates best with you and your goals.

8. **Consider Guided Sessions:** If you're unsure where to start, consider joining a beginner's yoga class or using online resources like instructional videos or apps that offer guided sessions. These can provide structure and guidance as you develop your practice.

9. **Set Realistic Goals:** Be patient with yourself and set achievable goals. Remember that progress in yoga is gradual, and the benefits often become more apparent over time.

By incorporating these tips into your journey, you can embark on a rewarding path of self-discovery and well-being through yoga, ultimately improving your stress levels and enhancing your sleep quality, even with short daily sessions.

Meditation

Meditation is categorized as a form of mind-body therapy because it often involves a fusion of mental and physical elements, such as deep breathing techniques. The goal of sleep meditation is to induce overall relaxation by addressing both anxious thoughts and physical stress symptoms, thereby preparing the body for restful sleep.

From a mental perspective, meditation techniques are designed to cultivate a more tranquil response to stress-inducing thoughts and emotions. Many meditation styles emphasize mindfulness, encouraging individuals to focus on the present moment with a non-judgmental mindset. Meditation can also involve concentration on repetitive phrases, visual imagery, sounds, or bodily sensations like breathing, all of which serve to reduce distractions.

Additionally, meditation aims to trigger a physical relaxation response that counteracts the body's stress response, commonly known as the "fight-or-flight" response. The stress response typically manifests as increased heart rate, rapid breathing, muscle tension, sweating, and elevated blood pressure—all of which hinder the ability to sleep. In contrast, the relaxation response induced by meditation leads to slower breathing, reduced heart rate and blood pressure, and a slowing of brainwave activity.

Mindfulness and meditation likely facilitate better sleep through various mechanisms:

- **Slowed Breathing:** Many meditation practices prioritize deep diaphragmatic breathing, which is associated with reduced anxiety. Focusing on calm, deep breathing is a primary way meditation alleviates anxiety.

- **Stress Pathway Regulation:** Meditation, like other relaxation techniques, can mitigate heart rate and blood pressure. Some evidence suggests that meditation diminishes the activation of stress-related pathways in the brain and lowers stress hormone levels.

- **Enhanced Mental Outlook:** By concentrating on the present moment, meditation can reduce rumination on past or future concerns, making individuals less reactive to challenging life events.

- **Pain Management:** While research results on pain reduction through meditation vary, it may enhance pain tolerance and make chronic pain more manageable, potentially aiding those who struggle to sleep due to pain.

Although further research is warranted, current evidence suggests that mindfulness meditation can enhance sleep quality to a degree comparable to exercise or cognitive behavioral therapy. Many individuals who participate in meditation programs report improved sleep quality even up to a year after the program's completion. Researchers attribute this improvement to alterations in brain connections, modifications in sleep stage transitions, and the practice of mental techniques that mitigate sleep-disrupting thoughts.

To maximize the potential benefits of meditation, it can be beneficial to incorporate it into a broader set of healthy sleep habits. This includes maintaining consistent bedtimes and creating a sleep-friendly environment that is cool, dark, and quiet.

How to Meditate

Meditation comes in various forms, each with its unique techniques. Nevertheless, most meditation practices share common principles:

• **Focus:** Meditation typically involves directing one's attention towards a specific object, a repetitive phrase, or their own breath. While maintaining this focus, individuals remain open to any passing thoughts but gently guide their awareness back to the chosen focal point in a non-judgmental manner.

• **Tranquil Setting:** Reducing external disturbances can assist meditators in achieving a serene mental state.

• **Deep Breathing:** Employing controlled, calm breathing patterns during meditation promotes relaxation. Practitioners are often encouraged to focus on engaging their diaphragm muscles located below the lungs, rather than relying on chest muscles.

• **Comfortable Posture:** Meditation can be conducted in a seated position, but it is also adaptable to standing, walking, lying down, or specific postures and movements.

Mindfulness Meditation

Mindfulness practices involve focusing on the present moment, enabling individuals to observe their emotions and thoughts without passing judgment. Similar to diaphragmatic breathing and progressive muscle relaxation, mindfulness can aid in relaxation prior to bedtime and alleviate symptoms of insomnia.

1. Guided Meditation

Guided meditation entails listening to an audio recording that guides one's thoughts during the meditation process. For instance, a guided meditation session might provide instructions on adjusting breathing, navigating through thoughts, or interpreting physical sensations. Guided imagery, a form of guided meditation, takes individuals on a visual journey to induce relaxation. It may include specific directions, such as imagining a walk along a tropical beach, engaging all five senses to immerse in the experience. Alternatively, it can be more open-ended, inviting individuals to envision their favorite place. Several studies have shown that guided meditation programs can enhance sleep quality.

2. Qigong

Qigong, a traditional Chinese medicine technique, employs mental focus, deliberate movements, and deep breathing to enhance the flow of energy within the body. Scientific evidence supporting the benefits of qigong is still emerging, with ongoing research exploring its potential to manage pain, improve overall quality of life, reduce stress and depression, and enhance sleep quality.

3. Tai Chi

Tai chi, a meditative practice characterized by continuous, gentle movements, was initially developed as a martial art but is currently used as a form of qigong to promote health and well-being. Practitioners of tai chi perform a series of postures at a slow, relaxed pace while concentrating on deep breathing and letting go of distracting thoughts.

4. Yoga

Yoga commonly incorporates elements of mindfulness meditation, diaphragmatic breathing, and stretching-based poses, with specific techniques varying based on the yoga style. Yoga instructors can recommend appropriate poses tailored to an individual's experience level, physical capabilities, and needs. Although limited high-quality research exists on the benefits of yoga, some studies suggest it may help reduce stress, enhance sleep quality, and address insomnia associated with stress or chronic health conditions.

5. Yoga Nidra

Also known as yogic sleep or psychic sleep, yoga nidra is a form of yoga designed to induce a sleep-like state. This state may mimic the brain waves occurring during sleep, including different sleep stages, while allowing individuals to maintain some level of consciousness. Yoga nidra incorporates elements like chanting, focused breathing, and awareness of various body parts. Research on yoga nidra's effects on sleep is still in its early stages, but preliminary studies suggest it may enhance sleep quality and reduce time spent awake in bed.

Pilates

Pilates, a gentle yet highly effective form of exercise, offers numerous benefits for reducing stress and improving sleep quality. This method, developed by Joseph Pilates in the early 20th century, focuses on enhancing core strength, flexibility, and overall body awareness. While it's primarily known for its physical advantages, Pilates also works wonders for mental and emotional well-being.

First and foremost, Pilates promotes stress reduction through mindful movement and controlled breathing. When you engage in Pilates exercises, you are encouraged to pay close attention to your breath and the sensations in your body. This mindfulness not only helps you to stay present in the moment but also calms your nervous system. Controlled breathing techniques, such as diaphragmatic breathing, can activate the body's relaxation response, reducing the production of stress hormones like cortisol.

Additionally, Pilates encourages the release of endorphins, which are natural mood elevators and stress reducers. As you engage in the exercises, your body releases these "feel-good" chemicals, leading to a sense of relaxation and well-being. This natural high can counteract the negative effects of stress and help you feel more at ease.

Furthermore, Pilates emphasizes gentle stretching and controlled movements, which can alleviate physical tension and stiffness commonly associated with stress. These exercises promote improved posture, flexibility, and muscle balance, all of which contribute to a greater sense of comfort and relaxation. By releasing tension in your muscles and joints, Pilates can help your body unwind, making it easier to cope with the physical manifestations of stress.

Pilates also enhances body awareness, teaching you to recognize and release areas of tension. This increased awareness can extend beyond the studio and into your daily life. When you are better attuned to your body's signals, you can identify and address stress triggers more effectively. You'll be more likely to notice when you're holding tension in your shoulders or clenching your jaw, for example, and take steps to relax those areas consciously.

Improved sleep quality is another significant benefit of Pilates. Stress often disrupts sleep patterns, leading to insomnia or poor-quality rest. Pilates, with its stress-reduction benefits, can indirectly improve sleep by helping you manage stress more effectively. When your mind is less cluttered with worries and your body is more relaxed, falling asleep and staying asleep becomes easier.

Moreover, Pilates can directly impact sleep by promoting relaxation and reducing physical discomfort. Stretching and gentle movements can relieve muscle tension, making it easier to get comfortable in bed. The improved posture and body awareness developed through Pilates can also alleviate issues like back pain that can disrupt sleep.

Consistent Pilates practice can also enhance the quality of your sleep by promoting a regular sleep schedule. The routine of attending Pilates classes or practicing at the same time each day can help regulate your body's internal clock, making it easier to fall asleep and wake up at the desired times.

Pilate Exercises

Several Pilates exercises can be particularly effective for reducing stress and improving sleep by promoting relaxation and body awareness. Here are some key Pilates exercises to consider:

1. **Diaphragmatic Breathing:** This is a fundamental Pilates exercise that focuses on deep, controlled breathing. Lie on your back with your knees bent then feet flat on the floor. Place one hand on your chest and the other on your abdomen. Take a deep breath in through your nose, letting your abdomen to expand as your lungs fill with air. Exhale gradually through your mouth, sensing your abdomen

contracting as you release the breath. This exercise helps activate the relaxation response, reducing stress and promoting calmness.

2. **Child's Pose Stretch:** Begin by positioning yourself on your hands and knees, then shift your weight back, settling onto your heels, and reach your arms forward. This gentle stretch helps release tension in the back, shoulders, and neck, areas often prone to stress-induced tightness. Hold this position while focusing on your breath for a couple of deep breaths.

3. **Cat-Cow Stretch:** Commence in a hands-and-knees position, and then alternate between rounding your back like a cat and arching it with your belly dropping toward the floor like a cow. This fluid motion helps improve spinal flexibility and relieves tension in the back and torso, contributing to a sense of relaxation.

4. **Rolling Like a Ball:** Sit on the floor with your knees pulled towards your chest then your hands holding your ankles. Round your spine into a C-curve and balance on your tailbone. Inhale as you roll back onto your shoulders, exhale to return to the starting position. This exercise massages the spine, relaxes the back muscles, and can be soothing.

5. **Legs Up the Wall:** While not a traditional Pilates exercise, this restorative yoga pose can complement your Pilates routine. Lie on your back with your legs extended up a wall, forming an L-shape with your body. This position encourages blood circulation and relaxation, making it easier to wind down and prepare for sleep.

6. **Savasana (Corpse Pose):** After your Pilates session, finish with Savasana. Lie flat on your back, arms by your sides, and legs mildly apart. Close your eyes and focus on your breath, releasing any residual tension. This relaxation pose can help calm the mind and prepare your body for restful sleep.

Remember that the key to using Pilates for stress reduction and improved sleep is to practice regularly and mindfully. Incorporate these exercises into your Pilates routine and use them as relaxation tools, paying close attention to your breath and sensations in your body. Over time, you'll likely experience reduced stress levels then improved sleep quality as a result of your Pilates practice.

Static Stretching

Static stretching is a simple and effective way to reduce stress and improve sleep quality. When you engage in static stretching, you perform slow and controlled movements that elongate and relax your muscles. This deliberate stretching activates your parasympathetic nervous system, which promotes a state of calm and relaxation, reducing stress and anxiety.

As you stretch, you release built-up tension in your muscles, which can help alleviate physical manifestations of stress, such as tightness in the neck, shoulders, and back. Additionally, static stretching can increase blood flow to your muscles, leading to improved circulation and a greater sense of well-being.

Furthermore, incorporating static stretching into your evening routine can enhance your sleep quality. Stretching prior to bedtime can relax your body and mind, making it easier to transition into a restful state. When you go to bed with relaxed muscles, you're more likely to experience deeper and more restorative sleep. This improved sleep quality not only helps reduce stress but also leaves you feeling more refreshed and energized the next day.

Static stretching is a simple yet powerful tool for stress reduction and better sleep. By incorporating static stretching exercises into your daily routine, especially prior to bedtime, you can experience the physical and mental benefits of reduced stress and improved sleep, leading to a healthier and more balanced life.

Static Stretching Exercise

Several static stretching exercises can help reduce stress and promote better sleep. Here are some effective stretches to consider incorporating into your daily routine:

Neck Stretch

1. Sit or stand with your back straight.

2. Softly incline your head to one side, directing your ear toward your shoulder.

3. Hold for 15-30 secs on all sides.

4. This stretch helps relieve tension in the neck and shoulders, reducing stress-related discomfort.

Shoulder Stretch

1. Extend one arm across your chest.

2. Use your opposite hand to gently pull your extended arm closer to your chest.

3. Hold for 15-30 secs on all sides.

4. This stretch releases tension in the shoulders and upper back, easing stress-related tightness.

Child's Pose

1. Start on your hands and knees.

2. Sit back on your heels, reaching your arms forward then lowering your chest toward the ground.

3. Hold for 30 secs to 1 min.

4. This yoga pose relaxes the entire body and calms the mind, making it beneficial for stress reduction and improved sleep.

Cat-Cow Stretch

1. Begin on your hands and knees.

2. Inhale as you arch your back (Cow pose), lifting your head and tailbone.

3. Exhale as you round your back (Cat pose), tucking your chin and tailbone.

4. Repeat for 1-2 mins.

5. This stretch helps relieve tension in the spine and promotes relaxation.

Seated Forward Bend

1. Sit with your legs extended in front of you.

2. Reach your arms toward your toes, bending at your hips.

3. Hold for 30 secs to 1 min.

4. This stretch stretches the lower back and hamstrings, relieving stress and promoting better sleep.

Butterfly Stretch

1. Sit with the soles of your feet touching each other, and your knees bent outward.

2. Gently press your knees toward the ground with your hands.

3. Hold for 30 secs to 1 min.

4. This stretch releases tension in the hips and groin, helping you relax prior to bedtime.

Legs Up the Wall Pose

1. Lie on your back with your legs extended up against a wall or headboard.

2. Relax your arms by your sides.

3. Hold for 5-10 mins.

4. This pose improves blood circulation, reduces leg swelling, and promotes a sense of calm and relaxation.

Deep Breathing Stretch

1. Sit or lie down comfortably.

2. Take slow, deep breaths in through your nose, expanding your diaphragm.

3. Exhale slowly through your mouth.

4. Continue for 5-10 mins.

5. Deep breathing blended with stretching helps reduce stress and prepare the body for restful sleep.

Incorporate these static stretches into your daily routine, especially in the evening, to reduce stress and prepare your body and mind for a good night's sleep. Remember to breathe deeply and focus on the sensation of the stretch to enhance the relaxation benefits.

Dynamic Stretching

Dynamic stretching is a form of exercise that involves active movements, often mimicking the motions of sports or activities. While its primary purpose is to improve flexibility and mobility, it can also play a significant role in reducing stress and promoting better sleep.

Dynamic stretching aids in stress reduction by enhancing blood circulation and delivering oxygen to muscles, thereby alleviating tension and fostering a sense of relaxation. Engaging in dynamic stretches also triggers the release of endorphins, our body's natural mood elevators, which can help alleviate stress and improve our overall mood.

Furthermore, dynamic stretching can enhance sleep quality. When we perform dynamic stretches, we engage various muscle groups and increase body temperature. After the stretching routine, the body gradually cools down, which can be conducive to falling asleep faster and experiencing deeper, more restful sleep. The reduction in muscle tension achieved through dynamic stretching can also prevent discomfort and restlessness during the night, promoting uninterrupted sleep.

Incorporating dynamic stretching into your daily routine, especially in the late afternoon or early evening, can have a positive impact on both stress reduction and sleep quality. It's an accessible and natural way to relax your body, alleviate stress, and prepare it for a restful night's sleep, ultimately contributing to overall well-being and health.

Dynamic Exercise

Dynamic stretching exercises that can help reduce stress and promote good sleep include:

1. **Arm Swings**: Stand with your feet at shoulder width and gently swing your arms forward and backward. This action aids in relieving tension in your shoulder and upper back muscles, promoting a sense of relaxation.

2. **Leg Swings**: Stand near a support, like a wall or chair, and swing one leg forward and backward in a controlled manner. This exercise helps loosen up your leg muscles and improves circulation.

3. **Hip Circles**: Stand with your feet at hip-width and perform circular motions with your hips, first in a clockwise and then in a counterclockwise direction. These movements can alleviate tension in your lower back and hip area.

4. **Torso Twists**: Stand with your feet shoulder-width apart and gently twist your torso from side to side. This exercise can alleviate tension in your spine and enhance flexibility.

5. **Neck Rolls**: Gently tilt your head from side to side and then roll it in a circular motion, both clockwise and counterclockwise. This can help relieve neck and shoulder tension, which is common when you're stressed.

6. **High Knees**: March in place while lifting your knees as high as possible. This exercise increases your heart rate mildly, helping to reduce stress, and it also improves circulation throughout your legs.

7. **Butt Kicks**: March in place while kicking your heels up towards your glutes. Like high knees, this exercise gets your heart rate up and promotes better circulation.

8. **Ankle Circles**: Sit on the floor or a chair and extend one leg. Rotate your ankle in a circular motion, first in a clockwise direction and then counterclockwise. This activity can aid in alleviating tension in your ankles and enhancing blood circulation to your lower limbs.

9. **Full Body Twists**: Stand with your feet hip-width apart and twist your entire body from side to side, allowing your arms to swing along with the motion. This exercise engages your core and can help release tension in your spine.

10. **Dynamic Breathing**: While standing or sitting with good posture, take slow, deep breaths, and coordinate your breath with arm movements. Inhale as you raise your arms overhead then exhale as you lower them. Focusing on your breath during dynamic stretches can calm your mind and reduce stress.

Perform these dynamic stretching exercises as part of your daily routine, particularly in the evening prior to bedtime. These movements help to relax your muscles, increase blood flow, release endorphins, and promote better posture and breathing, all of which contribute to reduced stress and improved sleep quality. Remember to perform them slowly and mindfully to maximize their benefits.

Download your bonus now, frame the QR code.
Quick Start Guide: Diet for Endomorphs

Conversion Table

Volume Equivalents (Liquid)

US Standard	US Standard (oz.)	Metric (approximate)
2 tbsps	1 fl. oz.	30 milliliter
¼ teacup	2 fl. oz.	60 milliliter
½ teacup	4 fl. oz.	120 milliliter
1 teacup	8 fl. oz.	240 milliliter
1½ teacups	12 fl. oz.	355 milliliter
2 teacups or 1 pint	16 fl. oz.	475 milliliter
4 teacups or 1 quart	32 fl. oz.	1 Liter
1 gallon	128 fl. oz.	4 Liter

Volume Equivalents (Dry)

US Standard	Metric (approximate)
⅛ tsp	0.5 milliliter
¼ tsp	1 milliliter
½ tsp	2 milliliter
¾ tsp	4 milliliter
1 tsp	5 milliliter
1 tbsp	15 milliliter
¼ teacup	59 milliliter
⅓ teacup	79 milliliter
½ teacup	118 milliliter
⅔ teacup	156 milliliter
¾ teacup	177 milliliter
1 teacup	235 milliliter
2 teacups or 1 pint	475 milliliter
3 teacups	700 milliliter
4 teacups or 1 quart	1 Liter

Oven Temperatures

Fahrenheit (F)	Celsius (C) (approximate)
250 deg.F	120deg.C
300 deg.F	150deg.C
325 deg.F	165deg.C
350 deg.F	180deg.C
375 deg.F	190deg.C
400 deg.F	200deg.C
425 deg.F	220deg.C
450 deg.F	230deg.C

Weight Equivalents

US Standard	Metric (approximate)
1 tbsp	15 gm
½ oz.	15 gm
1 oz.	30 gm
2 oz.	60 gm
4 oz.	115 gm
8 oz.	225 gm
12 oz.	340 gm
16 oz. or 1 lb.	455 gm

45 Days Meal Plan

Day	Breakfast	Lunch	Snack	Dinner
1	Veggie scramble	Baked Chicken and Vegetable Packets	Grilled Veggie Skewers	Seared Mahi-Mahi With Lemon Herb Sauce
2	Cottage cheese pancakes	Quinoa and Chickpea Salad	Baked Sweet Potato Fries	Blackened Salmon With Roasted Brussels Sprouts
3	Avocado and egg toast	Greek-Inspired Quinoa Salad	Roasted Chickpeas	Lemon Herb Baked Cod
4	Peanut Butter Banana Oatmeal	Teriyaki Tofu Stir-Fry	Grilled Asparagus Spears	Eggplant and Chickpea Curry
5	Overnight Chia Seed Pudding	Spinach and Feta Stuffed Chicken Breasts	Sautéed Spinach with Garlic	Mushroom and Spinach Quinoa Bowl
6	Spinach and Mushroom Omelet	Quinoa Stuffed Bell Peppers	Avocado and Tomato Salsa	Baked Turkey and Vegetable Foil Packets
7	Berry Protein Smoothie	Spaghetti Squash with Tomato Basil Sauce	Baked Eggplant Chips	Zucchini Noodles with Pesto
8	Greek Yogurt and Berry Parfait with Almonds	Balsamic Glazed Chicken with Roasted Vegetables	Roasted Brussels Sprouts	Teriyaki Salmon with Stir-Fried Bok Choy
9	Chia Seed Pudding	Stuffed Bell Peppers with Ground Turkey	Cabbage and Carrot Slaw	Turkey and Quinoa Stuffed Peppers
10	Sweet Potato and Spinach Hash	Lemon Garlic Shrimp and Zucchini Noodles	Greek Cucumber Cups	Eggplant and Zucchini Ratatouille

11	Cottage Cheese and Veggie Wrap	Chicken and Broccoli Stir-Fry	Sautéed Mushrooms with Garlic	Cauliflower Rice Stir-Fry with Tofu
12	Turkey and Spinach Breakfast Burrito	Mediterranean Chickpea Salad	Roasted Beet and Walnut Salad	Lentil and Vegetable Curry
13	Berry and Nut Butter Wrap	Quinoa and Black Bean Salad	Cucumber and Avocado Salsa	Greek Salad with Grilled Chicken
14	Mediterranean Scrambled Eggs	Lemon Herb Grilled Chicken Breasts	Steamed Artichoke with Lemon Herb Dipping Sauce	Baked Cod with Lemon and Herbs
15	Spinach and Tomato Breakfast Wrap	Spaghetti Squash with Tomato Basil Sauce	Roasted Radishes	Black Bean and Veggie Tacos
16	Almond Butter and Banana Smoothie	Stir-Fried Tofu and Broccoli	Cucumber and Radish Salad	Teriyaki Salmon with Stir-Fried Bok Choy
17	Veggie and Tofu Scramble	Eggplant Parmesan	Steamed Green Beans with Almonds	Greek Chicken and Vegetable Skewers
18	Turkey and Veggie Breakfast Casserole	Grilled Lemon Dill Salmon	Spicy Roasted Chickpeas	Baked Salmon with Asparagus
19	Quinoa Breakfast Bowl	Grilled Herb-Marinated Turkey Breast	Sautéed Spinach with Garlic	Lemon Herb Grilled Chicken Breasts
20	Spinach and Feta Breakfast Wrap	Thai-Inspired Tofu and Vegetable Stir-Fry	Avocado and Tomato Salsa	Lentil and Vegetable Curry
21	Oatmeal with Almonds and Berries	Chicken and Broccoli Stir-Fry	Roasted Chickpeas	Mushroom and Spinach Quinoa Bowl

22	Berry and Spinach Smoothie Bowl	Zucchini Noodles with Pesto	Baked Cauliflower Bites	Baked Turkey and Vegetable Foil Packets
23	Turkey and Spinach Breakfast Burrito	Baked Cod with Tomato and Olive Tapenade	Sautéed Mushrooms with Garlic	Teriyaki Tofu Stir-Fry
24	Greek Yogurt and Berry Parfait with Almonds	Spaghetti Squash with Tomato Basil Sauce	Lemon Garlic Roasted Chicken Thighs	Eggplant and Zucchini Ratatouille
25	Avocado and Egg Toast	Quinoa and Chickpea Salad	Steamed Broccoli with Lemon	Teriyaki Salmon with Stir-Fried Bok Choy
26	Veggie and Turkey Sausage Breakfast Casserole	Teriyaki Tofu Stir-Fry	Cucumber and Avocado Salsa	Cauliflower Rice Stir-Fry with Tofu
27	Quinoa Breakfast Bowl	Lemon Garlic Shrimp and Zucchini Noodles	Roasted Beet and Walnut Salad	Lentil and Vegetable Curry
28	Chia Seed Pudding	Stuffed Bell Peppers with Ground Turkey	Sautéed Spinach with Garlic	Greek Salad with Grilled Chicken
29	Spinach and Mushroom Breakfast Quesadilla	Mediterranean Chickpea Salad	Roasted Radishes	Black Bean and Veggie Tacos
30	Almond Butter and Banana Smoothie	Lemon Herb Grilled Chicken Breasts	Spicy Roasted Chickpeas	Baked Salmon with Asparagus
31	Veggie and Tofu Scramble	Greek-Inspired Quinoa Salad	Roasted Chickpeas	Lemon Herb Baked Cod
32	Spinach and Feta Breakfast Wrap	Balsamic Glazed Chicken with Roasted Vegetables	Avocado and Tomato Salsa	Eggplant and Chickpea Curry

33	Oatmeal with Almonds and Berries	Quinoa Stuffed Bell Peppers	Cabbage and Carrot Slaw	Baked Turkey and Vegetable Foil Packets
34	Berry and Spinach Smoothie Bowl	Spaghetti Squash with Tomato Basil Sauce	Baked Eggplant Chips	Zucchini Noodles with Pesto
35	Turkey and Veggie Breakfast Casserole	Teriyaki Tofu Stir-Fry	Steamed Artichoke with Lemon Herb Dipping Sauce	Teriyaki Salmon with Stir-Fried Bok Choy
36	Greek Yogurt and Berry Parfait with Almonds	Chicken and Broccoli Stir-Fry	Cucumber and Radish Salad	Lentil and Vegetable Curry
37	Peanut Butter Banana Oatmeal	Eggplant Parmesan	Steamed Green Beans with Almonds	Greek Chicken and Vegetable Skewers
38	Overnight Chia Seed Pudding	Thai-Inspired Tofu and Vegetable Stir-Fry	Avocado and Tomato Salsa	Teriyaki Tofu Stir-Fry
39	Veggie Scramble	Baked Cod with Tomato and Olive Tapenade	Sautéed Mushrooms with Garlic	Eggplant and Zucchini Ratatouille
40	Avocado and Egg Toast	Quinoa and Chickpea Salad	Roasted Beet and Walnut Salad	Lemon Herb Grilled Chicken Breasts
41	Turkey and Spinach Breakfast Burrito	Lemon Garlic Shrimp and Zucchini Noodles	Roasted Chickpeas	Black Bean and Veggie Tacos
42	Spinach and Tomato Breakfast Wrap	Lemon Herb Baked Cod	Greek Cucumber Cups	Teriyaki Salmon with Stir-Fried Bok Choy
43	Almond Butter and Banana Smoothie	Stuffed Bell Peppers with Ground Turkey	Spicy Roasted Chickpeas	Baked Salmon with Asparagus

44	Berry Protein Smoothie	Chicken and Broccoli Stir-Fry	Cabbage and Carrot Slaw	Eggplant and Chickpea Curry
45	Cottage Cheese Pancakes	Quinoa Stuffed Bell Peppers	Steamed Artichoke with Lemon Herb Dipping Sauce	Cauliflower Rice Stir-Fry with Tofu

Conclusion

In closing, "The Endomorph Diet for Beginners" has provided you with a comprehensive roadmap to unlock the full potential of your unique endomorphic body type. You've journeyed through the intricacies of tailored nutrition, effective fitness strategies, stress management techniques, and mindset shifts, all aimed at achieving not just weight loss but a holistic transformation of your life.

Throughout this book, you've discovered the power of embracing your genetic blueprint rather than fighting against it. You've gained valuable insights into the balanced intake of macronutrients, portion control, and the importance of nutrient-dense foods. The recipes have empowered you to create enjoyable and nourishing meals aligned with your body's specific needs.

The fitness routines tailored to endomorphs have shown you that exercise can be both effective and enjoyable, helping you boost your metabolism and sculpt your physique without extreme measures. Beyond diet and exercise, you've explored the vital role of stress management in your journey towards lasting health and vitality.

As you implement the principles of the endomorph diet into your life, remember that it's not just about shedding pounds; it's about embracing a holistic approach to well-being. By making informed food choices, engaging in suitable exercise routines, managing stress effectively, and cultivating a positive mindset, you can reshape your life for the better. The journey may have its challenges, but with the guidance and support provided in this book, you'll have the tools and knowledge you need to succeed.

In the end, the endomorph diet isn't a temporary fix but a sustainable lifestyle change. It's about working with your unique body type, not against it, to achieve lasting health and vitality. So, take the first step today, dive into the world of the endomorph diet, and discover the transformational power it holds for you. Your journey towards a healthier, more balanced life begins now.

Index

Stir-Fried Tofu and Broccoli; 36
Stuffed Bell Peppers with Ground Turkey; 39
Sweet Potato and Spinach Hash; 18
Teriyaki Salmon with Stir-Fried Bok Choy; 47
Teriyaki Tofu Stir-Fry; 37
Thai-inspired Tofu and Vegetable Stir-Fry; 37
Tuna and Cucumber Bites; 58
Turkey and Quinoa Stuffed Peppers; 48
Turkey and Spinach Breakfast Burrito; 27

Turkey and Spinach Stuffed Bell Peppers; 51
Turkey and Sweet Potato Hash; 52
Turkey and Vegetable Skillet; 40
Turkey and Veggie Breakfast Burrito; 19
Veggie and Tofu Scramble; 25
Veggie and Turkey Sausage Breakfast Casserole; 20
Veggie Scramble; 24
Zucchini Noodles with Pesto; 41

Printed in Great Britain
by Amazon

40340420R00057